THE NAZI
Connection to
ISLAMIC
Terrorism

THE NAZI
Connection to
ISLAMIC
Terrorism

Adolf Hitler and
Haj Amin al-Husseini

Chuck Morse

WND Books

THE NAZI CONNECTION TO ISLAMIC TERRORISM
WND Books

Published by WorldNetDaily
Washington, D.C.

JACKET DESIGN BY LINDA DALY
INTERIOR DESIGN BY NEUWIRTH & ASSOCIATES, INC.

WND Books are distributed to the trade by:
Midpoint Trade Books
27 West 20th Street, Suite 1102
New York, NY 10011

WND Books are available at special discounts for bulk purchases. WND Books, Inc. also publishes books in electronic formats. For more information call (541-474-1776) or visit www.wndbooks.com.

ISBN 13 Digit: 978-1-935071-03-7

Library of Congress information available

Printed in the United States of America

10 9 8 7 6 5 4 3 2 1

Endorsements

"Islam was once the most tolerant civilization on the planet. The House of Islam was the center for philosophical inquiry, science, poetry, and architecture. Islam left Christendom at the starting gate when it came to toleration of the other. But in recent decades, most of the Moslem world outside Turkey has become the center for xenophobia, violence, terrorism, Islamo-fascism, and barbarism. Chuck Morse tells one of the most revolting chapters in that tragic metamorphosis. It is one that must be learned by us all—those in the West now threatened by Islamo-fascism and jihad terrorism, and also those Moslems seeking to restore to the Islamic world its former laurels and humanism."

Prof. Steven Plaut, University of Haifa

"The greatest threat to Western civilization is radical Islam, which incorporates many of the ideological underpinnings of Nazism. In his new book, *The Nazi Connection to Islamic Terrorism*, Chuck Morse exposes how this phenomenon has come to dominate the political land-scape of the beginning of the twenty-first century. It is an historical breakthrough in understanding the link between Nazism and radical Islam. Morse details the key figures in this transition, the Muslim Brotherhood of Egypt and the mufti of Jerusalem, Haj Amin al-Husseini, who spent years in Germany synthesizing Arab Nationalism and Nazism."

**Rachel Neuwirth is a Los Angeles-based analyst
on the board of directors of the West Coast Region
of the American Jewish Congress and the chairperson
of the organization's Middle East committee.**

This book is dedicated to the memory of my cousin
Phillip Lerman

Contents

APPENDICES

Introduction

I wrote this book in response to the Islamic terrorist attack of September 11, 2001. That vicious attack woke America up to the terrorism that Israel has known since before the founding of the Jewish State in 1948.

A year before 9/11, a date which will live in infamy, the Camp David Talks, which were supposed to conclude the Oslo Peace process, had collapsed in a hail of dismembered body parts. The Camp David talks of 2000 were hosted by President Bill Clinton. At those talks the Israeli negotiating team, led by Israeli Prime Minister Edud Barak, offered to the Palestinian negotiating team, led by Palestinian Authority President Yasir Arafat, 97 percent of the territories commonly referred to as the West Bank and Gaza. Additionally, at those negotiating sessions the Israelis offered the Palestinians a piece of land inside the Israeli capital city of Jerusalem, border adjustments that would have resulted in Palestinian sovereignty over the equivalent of 100 percent of the area located within the 1949 Armistice lines, and permission for a number of Palestinians, the number to be determined, to move into Israel, the so-called right of return.

The Palestinians responded to the Camp David offer with suicide bombers at the Dolphin discothèque in Tel Aviv, at a Sbarro pizza parlor in Jerusalem, at a Tel Aviv shopping mall filled with young children shopping for Purim costumes, on busses, at a hotel in Netanya hosting a family attending a Passover Seder, and at Hebrew University.

Several years later, in 2003, Israeli Prime Minister Ariel Sharon handed over Gaza, ethnically cleansed of all of its Jews, to the Palestinian Authority. The Palestinians were handed a golden opportunity to turn that prime piece of beachfront property into a prosperous state, a Middle East version of Hong Kong, a responsible member of the community of nations. Besides handing over Gaza on a silver platter to the Palestinians with no preconditions, Israel once again, as it had done during the Oslo 1990s, provided money, supplies, and training for the Palestinians to help them to build a state, as did the American taxpayers. After the Israeli withdrawal from Gaza, the Palestinian Authority was scheduled to receive significant aid and investment from around the world, including money from many of the vast and oil-rich Arab and Islamic nations. Had Gaza chosen to conduct itself as a responsible nation, had Gaza chosen the path of peace, the Israelis were prepared to give the Palestinians a great deal more. There would have been a successful and peaceful Palestinian state on the West Bank and Gaza today if it had chosen peace, a state within the borders of present day Israel.

But instead the Palestinians of Gaza chose Hamas, which proceeded to turn Gaza into a launching pad for aggressive and unprovoked war against the State of Israel. The Gaza state in the making proceeded to fire thousands of deadly missiles over its border and into Israeli cities and towns, and it abducted Gilad Shalit, an Israeli soldier on Israeli soil. These are the facts.

I supported the Oslo Peace Process with great reluctance in the 1990s. While I did not believe the approach of land for peace would work, while I did not believe that by amputating an arm Israel would be able to save the life of the whole body, like a lot of Jews I nevertheless was sickened by the carnage. I could not stand the thought of reading another newspaper report about another Jewish man, women, child, elder, Holocaust survivor blown to bits because they dared to live their life in Israel. I could not bear to hear about another Jewish mother witnessing her baby stroller being blown up by a bomb. Like many, I was willing to suspend incredulity, to turn a blind eye, in order to ask Israel to go chasing after a piece of paper that had the word "peace" written upon it.

At this time I can no longer support the Oslo process. I believe the process is dead. There must not be another Palestinian state, at least not one that would be carved out of that tiny swath of land that rests uneasily between the Jordan River and the Mediterranean Sea. There are already two Palestinian states, a Jewish one and an Arab one, Israel and Jordan. There are already over twenty Arab states, many of them soaked in oil and natural resources. Another state within Israel's present border would spell national suicide for Israel. This book is an examination of the nature of the conflict between Israel and the Arabs going back to the establishment of the British Mandate of Palestine in 1920.

Many leaders of movements, religious, political, or cultural, leave their marks on history and on the lives and actions of their followers, and this influence at times endures for generations, even millennia. This is true, for example, regarding the faith, philosophy, style, and even the appearance and mannerisms of great figures such as Moses, Jesus, Mohammed, and Buddha. This is also true about more modern leaders such as George Washington, Karl Marx, Abraham Lincoln, Franklin D. Roosevelt, Martin Luther King, and Ronald Reagan. We study these leaders not only to obtain insight into their thinking but also to gain insight into the nature of their influence on our own times and on the movements that carry on their legacy.

This is why it is important to study the life and work of Haj Amin al-Husseini, known as the grand mufti of Jerusalem and widely considered to be the founding father of the modern Palestinian movement. Al-Husseini was both a religious and a political figure; he held the religious office of mufti of Jerusalem and he simultaneously held the political office of head of the Supreme Muslim Council in British Palestine in the 1920s and early 1930s. Likewise the conflict between the Jews and the Arabs in Israel is also both political and religious. Al-Husseini's policies, and his beliefs and actions would set the tone for how the Arab leaders and populations of Palestine, and indeed of most of the Arab world, would respond to the aspirations of sovereignty held by the Jews in Palestine.

Evidence suggests that al-Husseini was not only an anti-Zionist but also an anti-Semite as the term is used to describe those who generally hate Jews. Al-Husseini would tolerate Jews in Palestine only if they accepted *dhimmi* status, which is as second-class citizens with no rights. The traditional status of *dhimmi* in the Arab world, generally applied to non-Muslims living in the Arab world, was analogous to the status afforded to African-Americans in Southern American society before the Civil Rights Movement.

Al-Husseini initiated the tactic of suicide bombing in the 1930s not against Jews, but against Palestinian Arabs willing to talk to Jews. This raises an interesting question, which is: Why did the Western democracies, first Britain and then the United States, so often support the more radical elements in the Middle East and often at the expense of the more moderate element? It was the British governor-general of Palestine, Sir Herbert Samuel, who installed al-Husseini as mufti of Jerusalem in spite of his having been previously convicted of instigating a murderous riot against Jews in Jerusalem and in spite of his losing a plebiscite for the position of mufti that was held among the Arab citizens of Palestine. Moderate Arabs who were willing to work peacefully alongside a modest Jewish state, a state that would recognize and protect the rights of Arabs and Muslims, would be ignored, driven out of public life, and sometimes murdered, and this remains the case to this day in the Palestinian community.

The appendix of this book contains the virtually forgotten Faisal-Weizmann Agreement in which the moderate post–World War I Arab leader King Faisal ibn Hussein of Syria signed an accord with Chaim Weizmann, head of the Zionist movement in London in 1919. This author contends that this far-sighted agreement represents international law. The Hashemite King Faisal, considered to have been a direct descendent of the Prophet Mohammed as well as the political leader of the Arab world after World War I, wrote that the return of the Jews to their ancient homeland was consistent with his Muslim faith and was in the best interest of the emerging Arab nations achieving independence from Turkey and from the European colonial powers. Faisal envisioned a partnership between Jew and Muslim, Israel and the Arab states, as they moved together into the new modern era of national sovereignty. Haj Amin al-Husseini had different ideas and would play a significant role in overturning Faisal's progressive vision.

Al-Husseini was the first leader to send a congratulatory letter to Adolf Hitler upon his election in 1933. In 1936, al-Husseini contacted Nazi emissary Adolf Eichmann during his visit to Palestine and Egypt. Soon after, al-Husseini became a paid agent of the Nazis and instigated a revolt against the British in Palestine. After the British evicted him from Palestine he moved on to Iraq, where he played a behind-the-scenes role in a pro-Nazi coup in 1940 and a role in the Fahud, the anti-Jewish pogrom that followed the collapse of the pro-Nazi Iraqi coup.

After fleeing Iraq, and after stopping in Tehran, Istanbul, and Rome, al-Husseini ended up in Berlin where he held a well-publicized meeting with Hitler. At that meeting, Hitler promised to set al-Husseini up as a Nazi führer in the Middle East after he subdued Europe. The plan was for al-Husseini to lead Nazi-Muslim brigades across the Caucasus Mountains where they would impose a Nazi-Muslim caliphate. Hitler and al-Husseini also discussed "the Jewish problem."

Al-Husseini was the de facto head of a Nazi-Muslim government-in-exile in Berlin during the war. He conducted bone-chilling anti-Semitic broadcasts, was financed by money confiscated from Jews after they were sent to the death camps, was involved in training Bosnian Muslim Hanzar brigades to fight for the Nazi Wehrmacht, and he initiated espionage and sabotage in the Middle East against the Allies and against the Jews of Palestine. Al-Husseini toured the death camps and sent letters to pro-Nazi European leaders urging them to send their Jews to "Poland," which was a euphemism for the crematoria. There are many incidences known in which al-Husseini was more pro-Nazi and more of a promoter of the Holocaust than were the Nazi elite themselves.

Al-Husseini was never held to account for his World War II crimes, as he slipped out of Germany one step ahead of a summons to appear at the Nuremberg Tribunal. He went on to Cairo where he operated against Israel with a virtual free hand until his death in 1975. He assisted in the smuggling of Nazi war criminals into the Middle East, where many of them converted to Islam, adopted Muslim names, and rose to positions of prominence in Arab capitals. He played a role in training irregulars, including Yasir Arafat, who was purported to be his nephew, to fight against Israel in its war of independence. There were reports of men on the front line attacking Israel in Hanzar uniforms.

Al-Husseini briefly headed an all-Arab government in Gaza and called for Arabs to leave Israel with promises that they would be returned. He was implicated in the assassination of the moderate Jordanian King Abdallah, who wanted peace with Israel, and he played a major role in instituting Arab refugee camps by discouraging Arab governments from assimilating the Arab refugees for political reasons.

Remaining an Islamic extremist and a Nazi for the rest of his life, it could be argued that Haj Amin al-Husseini is also the father of the modern jihadist movement against the Western democracies and against the moderate Arab and Muslim countries.

The Palestinian Arabs and their supporters make a legitimate and reasoned argument in terms of why they should be sovereign in Palestine west of the Jordan River. This simple fact should be acknowledged and should not be denied. Both sides have been locked in an interminable debate that goes around and around in circles. To argue the Israeli-Arab conflict is like being trapped on a merry-go-round. While this author recognizes the legitimacy of the Palestinian Arab position, the sincerity in which they hold that position, and the sacrifices they have made in preserving their position, it is nevertheless contended here, with respect, that the Palestinian Arab position, while legitimate, is simply not as strong as the Israeli position on all levels. So what then should be done?

For political reasons Israel should openly declare that there will be no further withdrawal from the territory in which it now resides. The Arab populations of Gaza, Judea, and Samaria should be granted regional autonomy and should establish governments modeled after the canton system of Switzerland. Arabs residing in the cantons should have the option of receiving Israeli citizenship and passports that list them as dual citizens of both Israel and their respective cantons. Israel should invest in these cantons economically and work toward improving the quality of life for the Arab residents. Jews should be permitted to live anywhere they choose to live inside Israel.

It should be declared, openly and unapologetically, that Israel is the Jewish state and that the primary mission of Israel is to serve as the homeland of the Jewish people. While the rights of the minority population and minority religions must be respected, as would be in accord with Jewish tradition, the State of Israel should nevertheless unabashedly promote its Jewish identity. Israel should continue to hold out the olive branch of peace to all Arab and Muslim nations and peoples and, in accord with the Faisal-Weizmann Agreement, Israel should continue to seek to develop cultural, economic, and trade alliances with the Arab world for the benefit of all.

I am now going to venture very carefully into some highly speculative and controversial opinions, so be forewarned. Israel, supported by

Jews from around the world, should take steps to offer Arab residents of Israel financial incentives to emigrate to other Arab or non-Arab nations. This is not ethnic cleansing, as this would be a strictly voluntary program and would be handled on a case-by-case basis. No person or family would ever be required to leave Israel or suffer any repercussions from staying in Israel. This privately run and funded program should be accompanied by increased efforts to encourage Jewish immigration into Israel, particularly from African and Asian countries. For practical reasons, Israel cannot retreat into the rump state with truncated borders that existed before the Six-Day War of 1967. To do so would be a regressive turn backward and would engender the same problems Israel confronted in those difficult years.

I acknowledge that I am about to enter into extreme controversy by dipping my toe into the very contentious waters of a brief examination of the religious claims surrounding the conflict. It cannot be denied that religion plays a central role in the conflict and to ignore this factor would be presenting an incomplete picture. The fact is that Israel today exists in exactly the land that was promised to the Jews by the Almighty, promised to Abraham, Isaac, Jacob, and to the children of Israel in the Torah. This would be the modest land that lies within the region between the Jordan River to the east and the (Mediterranean) Great Sea to the west, from Dan (Mount Hermon) to the north to Beersheba to the south. In fact, the only part of Israel that was not specifically promised to the children of Israel by the Almighty in the Torah but that is a part of modern Israel today is the slice of desert that runs from Beersheba south to the Red Sea and to the Israeli port city of Eilat.

Yet the religious claims of Islam to Israel are also quite real and emotional. Besides the existence of Islamic holy sites within Israel, sites that the Israelis have been meticulous to leave in Islamic hands, the land itself has a sense of holiness that makes it a coveted piece of real estate not just for Jews and Muslims but also for Christians. I am presenting a proposal here that will probably satisfy nobody, but I humbly present it just the same. The fact is that the Jews lost all effective sovereignty over Israel in 70 AD when the Romans destroyed the Second Temple. That sovereignty was miraculously restored in 1948. The Temple Mount today remains holy to both Jews and Muslims.

The Book of Kings makes reference to Hiram, the king of Tyre, and the partnership he formed with King Solomon in the building of the

Temple in Jerusalem. The Book of Kings also makes reference to another Hiram, son of a widow of the tribe of Naphtali, whose father was of Tyre and who served as a master architect and builder of the Temple. It seems clear from the text that Solomon worked in close collaboration with Hiram of Tyre, a king of a great Canaanite city, in the building of the Temple.

Perhaps this Biblical story might serve as a model for a Jewish-Islamic project to rebuild the Temple on the Temple Mount in Jerusalem today. Ultimately, only the Almighty will know the right time and the right circumstance to rebuild the Temple, but I propose that a committee be formed, made up equally of Jewish rabbis and Muslim imams, that would agree to study the issue for a period of no less than seventy years. Seventy men, selected to serve on the committee by their respective religious peers, would serve ten-year terms. The committee would be made up of thirty-five rabbis and thirty-five imams, respected men of high morals and high levels of learning. The presidency would rotate between a rabbi and an imam. The committee would meet in secret but would occasionally issue reports on their progress and reflections. As the end of the seventy years approaches, the committee would decide whether it required another seventy-year extension to examine the issue. With the help of the Almighty, and with the prayers of both Jews and Muslims, the Temple would be rebuilt under the direction of both the children of Israel and the children of Ishmael and this would serve, G-d willing, as a sign of a new era of peace.

THE **NAZI**
Connection to
ISLAMIC
Terrorism

The Nazi Holocaust Continues

The Nazi Holocaust against the Jews of Europe did not end with the collapse of Nazi Germany in 1945, but rather the genocidal program of Holocaust has continued against the Jews of Israel. Hitler's crematoria have been replaced by human bombs, programmed to blow themselves up for the sole purpose of killing as many Jews as possible. Instead of thousands lining the streets of German cities saluting and sig-heiling, thousands, with their heads wrapped in scarves, rally and chant menacingly in Arab and Muslim cities.

Nazi-style anti-Semitism continues on its grim goose-step across the Arab and Islamic landscape as Arab and Muslim nations promulgate, through their media outlets, their public institutions, and their schools, the same hateful and demented anti-Jewish conspiracy theories as did Hitler. Anti-Semitism is as much a state-sponsored article of faith in many Muslim capitals today as it was in wartime Berlin over six decades ago.

Many Arab and Islamic governments continue to emulate the Nazi system itself, a system that was a toxic amalgam of anti-Semitism, socialism, hyper-nationalism, and imperialism. Militaristic and authoritarian

Arab and Islamic governments continue to repress any move toward democracy, private property, individual rights, freedom of expression, and the development of a prosperous middle class.

Germany was one of the richest nations in Europe, yet, under the Nazis, the impulse to run roughshod over weaker neighbors and impose an iron fist across Europe proved irresistible. Thus is the case with the vast and oil-rich sovereign Arab and Islamic states who seem unable to live peacefully with most of their non-Islamic neighbors but instead aggressively pursue a policy of imposing their will on what Harvard professor Samuel Huntington accurately referred to as "Islam's bloody borders." Arab petro-dollars fund militias and terror cells that are set up to terrorize non-Muslim nations.

Was the Nazi Holocaust against the Jews literally transplanted into the Middle East from Nazi Germany? This book attempts to connect the dots by analyzing the career of Palestinian Arab leader Haj Amin al-Husseini (1895-1974) and his direct relationship with Hitler and the Nazis. Al-Husseini was not the only Muslim leader to collaborate with the Nazis, and there was general sympathy for the Nazis throughout the Middle East in the 1930s. The Nazi program, in fact, had a profound and enduring influence on Muslim politics and culture. An understanding of that influence goes a long way toward understanding the political crisis of today.

If a date could be fixed to the launching in earnest of the Nazi Holocaust against the Jews of Europe, that date would be November 25, 1941. On that date, Adolf Hitler met with al-Husseini in Berlin. At that well-documented meeting, Hitler promised al-Husseini, acting in his capacity as a Palestinian pan-Arab leader, that once the Nazis secured a dominant military position in Europe, they would proceed to send the Wehrmacht, the Nazi war machine, on a blitzkrieg across the Caucasus and into the Arab world. Hitler revealed his long-range plans to al-Husseini, which included the creation of a Nazi-Muslim-dominated Middle East. He stated that he intended to accomplish this while posing as the liberator of the Arabs from British occupation.

According to notes taken at the meeting as well as al-Husseini's diary, Hitler promised the Arab leader that he would help in the creation of either a united Nazi-Muslim Middle East or the cobbling together of a federation of Nazi-Muslim puppet states, modeled after those the Nazis were establishing in Europe at the time. At that meeting, in which al-Husseini was treated with the type of pomp traditionally afforded an important visiting head of state, Hitler promised al-Husseini that he would be installed as the führer of a Nazi-Arab entity.

Records of this historic meeting, al-Husseini's diary, and an examination of the life and public utterances of al-Husseini over five decades lead to the reasonable conjecture that at their meeting, Hitler and al-Husseini discussed "the Jewish question," with Hitler likely filling al-Husseini in on the genocidal plan. Hitler did, in fact, promise al-Husseini, in explicit terms, that after the "final solution" against the Jews of Europe was accomplished, the Nazis would install him as the Muslim führer of the Middle East. Hitler promised al-Husseini that the time would come when the "final solution" against the Jews would be implemented in Palestine and eventually in the entire Arab world (*Appendix E*).

Less than two months after the Hitler-al-Husseini meeting, the infamous Wannsee Conference took place in a suburb of Berlin. At this conference, high-level Nazi officials set in motion the mechanics of the genocidal program that sealed the fate of most of the Jews of Nazi-occupied Europe. Hitler's promises to al-Husseini regarding a Nazi-Muslim Middle East would be postponed and would never come to pass, as by 1945 the Nazis were utterly crushed by the Allied powers.

Having spent the war years in Berlin, where he was treated as a virtual head of a Nazi-Muslim government-in-exile, al-Husseini fled Europe at the end of the war, one step ahead of the Nuremberg tribunal. Al-Husseini settled in Cairo after having been tipped off that he was about to be charged with crimes against humanity by Yugoslavia and Hungary. While European Nazism was delegated to the sewers of history by the heroic and victorious Allies, a form of Nazism, largely introduced by al-Husseini and his followers, and furthered by his wartime collaboration with Hitler and the Nazi regime, continues on its long goose-step toward the hybrid National Socialist-style Muslim movement that dominates in many Middle Eastern countries today.

In post–World War II Cairo, al-Husseini established himself as a key player in an ongoing and successful effort to transfer aspects of Hitler's program of genocide against the Jews into the Middle East and into the Arab conflict with the new State of Israel. Israel achieved sovereignty in

1948, a mere three years after the end of the Nazi Holocaust and the European war. Al-Husseini and his entourage of pro-Nazi Arabs, many of whom had spent the war years with him in Berlin, along with German Nazis fleeing from justice and settling in Arab capitals, proceeded to set up shop in the Arab countries. The politics, personality, and career of this one man, Haj Amin al-Husseini, sheds light on the true nature of what has metastasized into a radical Islamo-fascism that now poses a threat not only to Israel but also to moderate Muslims and to the entire non-Muslim world.

Known for his traditional manners and unassuming charisma, Amin al-Husseini was a fully committed, ruthless, and totally dedicated fanatic. By the sheer force of his personality, al-Husseini proved to be a key player in terms of introducing Nazi culture and politics into the Arab world before, during, and after the war. Consequently, al-Husseini, by his actions during a career that spanned over five decades, would be the primary instigator of the Israel-Arab conflict, both before and after Israeli independence, and, by extension, the ongoing conflict between radical Islam and the non-Muslim nations and peoples of the world. These conflicts were by no means preordained.

Al-Husseini played a significant role in the development of Nazi-style political organizations in Palestine as well as in other Arab capitals. He funneled money that had been confiscated from the Jews of Europe by the Nazis, using the funds to finance anti-Jewish and anti-Israel activities before, during, and after the war. He played a direct and significant role in the Holocaust against the Jews of Europe. He was involved in the recruitment of Nazi-Muslim SS brigades in Nazi-occupied Europe. After the war, he helped to establish postwar links between Nazis and Arabs. This busy man was a leader in terms of exporting Nazism to the Middle East, where it has since morphed into what has been often and appropriately called muftism, in honor of his infamy.

Palestinian Arabs today consider al-Husseini to be the founding father of their movement, yet the evidence presented in this book indicates that it would not be an exaggeration to suggest that it was Adolf Hitler himself who was as much the founder of the Palestinian movement as was al-Husseini. Al-Husseini first placed his indelible imprimatur on the ongoing conflict between the Jews and the Arabs in 1920, when he instigated a slaughter of Jewish settlers in Palestine. From that point on, he would lead in the development of an Islamic terror network that now reaches global proportions. Today, the followers of the movement that al-Husseini played an instrumental role in creating have declared themselves to be at war with the entire non-Muslim world.

In the process of introducing terror into the modern Middle East, al-Husseini played a significant role in promoting a particularly virulent strain of fundamentalist Islam. National socialism, and later communism, as embraced by the Islamists, would lend a modern pseudo-scientific gloss to certain ancient ideas contained within Islam and al-Husseini was a major bridge figure in that transformation. There should be no question about the fact that al-Husseini was one of the most rabid and vicious anti-Semites in history. His name should be enshrined in the same rogues gallery of Jew haters as Pharaoh, Haman, Antiochus, Titus, Hadrian, Chmielnicki, and, of course, Hitler, with whom he was a collaborator.

Al-Husseini began his public career in the immediate aftermath of World War I, upon returning to his native Jerusalem after serving in the Ottoman Turkish Army. Al-Husseini would work tirelessly throughout his life, until his death in 1974, to advance a single-minded agenda, which was the complete eradication of the Jewish settlers in Palestine. He never once compromised with the Jews of Palestine in his insistence that every last one of them be expelled. He never once even met with the Jews, and this fanatical refusal to even recognize the most basic aspect of their existence has been a hallmark of the movement he would spawn. In his adamant refusal to recognize any national rights whatsoever for the Jews in Palestine, and his insistence that Palestine be rendered virtually *judenrein*, he would actually be responsible for losing many opportunities for the Arabs to achieve a large measure of sovereignty west of the Jordan River. That intransigent position on the part of al-Husseini remains a mainstay and a driving force among radical Arabs to this day.

My contention is that the legacy of al-Husseini is a regressive embrace on the part of many Arab and Islamic nations and peoples of an unholy amalgam of a fundamentalist form of Islam and of the national socialism of Hitler. The contention of this book is that the ideas and tactics introduced into the Arab world by al-Husseini and his associates are largely in ascendance in many of today's Arab and Islamic countries. This book is an examination of those ideas and how they manifested themselves in al-Husseini's career, as well as an examination of the destructive influence his legacy has had for Arabs.

Amin al-Husseini was an authoritarian-minded pan-Arab leader who believed in the old and imperialistic utopian Muslim notion that the disciples of the Prophet Mohammed must work toward the creation of a single and solitary united Arab caliphate, which would serve as the central governing authority over Islam and ultimately the entire world. He embraced a fundamental tenet of Islam, which contends that the establishment of such a caliphate would lead to Dar el-Islam, or a world under Islam. This idea, one that runs as a strand throughout Arab and Islamic history, was by no means predestined to take hold in the immediate post–World War I Middle East.

This imperialistic notion was not unlike contemporary Western imperialist utopian movements that emerged after World War I, such as communism, which sought a world under socialism, and Nazism, which sought what Hitler referred to as a new social order and a thousand-year Reich. Certainly al-Husseini found himself in the company of many similar minds and movements of his day, movements with similar world aspirations.

In those halcyon, post–World War I years, a time when al-Husseini was launching his public career, Arabs were taking their first tentative steps toward national sovereignty and individual rights after having suffered for over four hundred years under the stultifying occupation of the Turkish Ottoman Empire. There was a great sense of exhilaration and much hope and expectation among Arabs in the waning years of Ottoman power. These hopes, contained within the breasts of many Arabs, were that the Arab nations would emerge from the desolation of Ottoman rule and would join the modern world as fully sovereign partners. Many Arabs were excited over the bright prospect of enjoying all of the modern benefits of fast-developing technologies, communication, free market economy, and democracy.

Many enlightened and genuinely progressive Arab leaders during this period sought peace and freedom for their people. A most exemplary figure of this mindset, certainly not the only one, was the Emir Faisal ibn Hussein, the son of Hussein bin Ali, sharif of Mecca and later king of Hijaz. Faisal and his family, known as the Hashemites, were generally considered by Arabs to be direct descendents of the Prophet Mohammed, and Faisal was one of the most respected leaders in the Arab world at the time. Faisal would become the formally recognized head of the Arab delegation at the Paris Peace Conference, which was held in 1919 at the end of World War I. Faisal would go on to become first king of Syria and then king of Iraq and his brother, Abdallah, also a progressive, would become king of Palestine east of the Jordan, or Transjordan. The Paris Peace Conference, which drew up the Treaty of Versailles, ending the long and bloody European war, would also define the postwar world by setting precedence in international law, by recognizing new and sovereign nations, and by establishing the League of Nations.

Emir Faisal, as the accredited head of the Arab delegation to the Paris Peace Conference, sought recognition by the League of Nations of the national and political rights and aspirations of the twenty-two Arab nations that were emerging from the Ottoman ruins. In exchange for this recognition from the international community, Faisal formally recognized a British Mandate for a Jewish Palestine in 1918. The League of Nations had organized and recognized a British Mandate for Palestine, and that mandate was supposed to facilitate in the development of a Jewish national home. Faisal signed an agreement recognizing the British Mandate in the name of the Arab world and the agreement that he signed, I would contend, carries the weight of international law. This astonishing agreement, known as the Faisal-Weizmann Agreement, is virtually unknown today, and for some strange reason, the agreement is rarely, if ever, discussed in diplomatic circles (*Appendix C*).

The Balfour Declaration had been previously issued by the British, in 1917, during the darkest days of the world conflagration, and that declaration constituted a formal recognition by Great Britain of a Jewish national home in Palestine (*Appendix A*). The Balfour Declaration would also be incorporated as a formal part of the League of Nations charter, which established a British Mandate for Palestine as a temporary entity created for the express purpose of supporting the goals of the Balfour Declaration. Most of the nations of the world had also accepted the Balfour Declaration by 1918. My contention is that the Faisal-Weizmann Agreement constitutes a formal recognition by the Arab authorities of the Balfour Declaration and its goals and therefore constituted Arab recognition of Jewish Palestine.

On January 3, 1919, in London, the Emir Faisal ibn Hussein signed the formal agreement with his diplomatic counterpart, Dr. Chaim Weizmann, who was at that time acting as the head of the World Zionist Organization and who was also acting in his capacity as the accredited and recognized head of the Zionist delegation to the Paris Peace Conference (*Appendix C*). Additionally, in subsequent correspondence with Harvard Law School Professor and future Supreme Court Justice Felix Frankfurter (*Appendix B*), Faisal accurately referred to Jewish claims in Palestine as "modest and proper" and offered the Jewish people "a hearty welcome home." Such language and sentiments coming from as eminent and revered a figure as Faisal, sentiments common among many Arabs at the time, would be almost unthinkable today as a result, primarily, of the influence of this one man, the grand mufti of Jerusalem, Haj Amin al-Husseini.

Emir Faisal, like many enlightened Arab leaders of his era, accurately and prudently believed that the newly emerging post–World War I Arab nations could and ought to benefit from the economic know-how and the modern European experience of the Jewish settlers in Palestine. Faisal was certainly a nationalist, in the best meaning of the term, and as such he wanted the Arabs to become full and sovereign partners in the modern world and to take their rightful place among the emerging nations of the world. Faisal felt that a relationship with a Jewish Palestine would be of great benefit in achieving these goals and he also seemed to have a well-developed sense of fairness, high-mindedness, and compassion to go along with his basic common sense. In retrospect, it is hard to believe, after all the subsequent conflicts and violence between the Jews of Israel and the Arab nations and peoples, that such an enlightened figure as Faisal once held sway in the Arab world. The dark influence of al-Husseini would come to largely eclipse that of the enlightened Faisal, to the detriment of both Jews and Arabs.

Haj Amin al-Husseini, who became the grand mufti of Jerusalem, made his grand debut on the world stage after having served as an artillery officer in the Central powers–allied Ottoman Turkish Army during World War I. Toward the end of that war, al-Husseini switched his allegiance from the Turks to the Allied side and returned to his native Palestine, now under British administration. In 1920, al-Husseini played a significant role in instigating the first large-scale pogrom against the Palestinian Jewish settlers. This pogrom represented the first time in hundreds of years that innocent Jews were slaughtered wholesale in the Arab world and marked the first bloodletting in what has been an ongoing conflict between the Jews and the Arabs ever since. Before the 1920 pogrom, a prevailing point of view among both the Arab and the Jewish settlers in Palestine was that the future of Palestine would be resolved with the establishment of some sort of a cooperative and shared state.

In 1921, shortly after the launching of the 1920 pogrom and for reasons that will forever remain shrouded in mystery, Sir Herbert Samuel, a British Jew who had been appointed by the British as high commissioner of the Palestine Mandate that same year, appointed al-Husseini as grand mufti of Jerusalem. This historic appointment, and subsequent appointments of al-Husseini to additional and more political positions in Palestine, was made in spite of vigorous protests coming from both the Jewish settlers and from the majority of the Palestinian Arabs. Al-Husseini proceeded, over the next several decades, to instigate violence against the Jews in Palestine, instill a hatred of the Jews throughout the Arab world, and to brutally purge and assassinate any Arab who dared to oppose him.

His followers and his many protégés continue in this tradition.

Al-Husseini sympathized with, and publicly embraced, the philosophy and goals of the Third Reich at the time of Adolf Hitler's ascension to power in 1933. In 1937, al-Husseini became the highest-ranking Arab leader to become directly involved with the Third Reich when he met face to face with Nazi Hauptscharführer Adolf Eichmann and SS Oberscharführer Herbert Hagen during their secretive visit to Palestine. Following this astonishing meeting, al-Husseini became, for all intents and purposes, a full-fledged Nazi in every sense of the word, as well as a paid agent of the Third Reich, according to testimony both at the Nuremberg tribunal and at the Eichmann trial. Al-Husseini's career after this fateful meeting is truly fascinating, although not widely known, and is the kind of stuff that couldn't be matched by the most adventurous work of fiction.

After being implicated by the British in the bloody 1937-1939 riots in Palestine, al-Husseini moved on to Lebanon, and then to Baghdad, where he helped to foment the pro-Nazi Rashid Ali officers' coup against the British government in Iraq in 1941. At this pivotal juncture in the war between the Nazis and the British, al-Husseini arranged for German funds and fighter-bombers to be employed in the support of the pro-Nazi Iraq coup plotters, known as the Golden Square. Nazi fighter-bombers would take off from airfields in pro-Nazi Vichy French Syria on their way to Iraq on bombing missions. After the coup failed, al-Husseini proceeded to flee to Rome, and then to Berlin, where he spent the remaining war years in the service of the Third Reich.

One of the Iraqi coup plotters, all of whom coordinated their efforts with al-Husseini, who was at the time acting as Hitler's agent, was General Khairallah Tulfah, who was also the uncle, guardian, mentor, and future father-in-law of Iraqi arch-dictator Saddam Hussein. Besides Saddam Hussein, al-Husseini would both directly and indirectly mentor several subsequent Arab leaders, intellectuals, and terrorists. Al-Husseini was also a mentor to Yasir Arafat, who has publicly praised him on many occasions, who shares his name, and who is believed by many to be al-Husseini's nephew.

Al-Husseini lived in Berlin during the World War II years, where he resided in the luxurious surroundings of a mansion confiscated from a wealthy Jew. The Nazis set al-Husseini up as a virtual head of a Nazi-Muslim government-in-exile and gave him access to what they called the *Sonderfund*, which was made up of money and property that had been confiscated from European Jews after they had been railroaded to the death camps. Besides spending the fund of confiscated money to support his lavish lifestyle and to offer gratuities to friends and allies, al-Husseini spent this confiscated Jewish money on, among other things, the launching of an international anti-Jewish, and, later, anti-Israel, propaganda campaign that continues to rage.

Upon his arrival in Berlin in 1941, al-Husseini met first with the Nazi foreign minister Joachim von Ribbentrop and then was officially received by Adolf Hitler on November 28. Less than two months after the al-Husseini-Hitler meeting, the Nazis held the Wannsee Conference, which launched the Holocaust against the Jews. Subsequently, and through the war years, the "Grossmufti vom Jerusalem," as he was known to the Nazis and to the German people, would meet regularly with high Nazi officials and would play a leading role, perhaps a more significant role than is commonly known or that will ever be entirely known, in the "final solution" against the Jews of Europe.

Al-Husseini was intimately involved in the recruiting and training of Bosnian Muslim SS Hanzar divisions in Nazi-occupied Yugoslavia and was also a leader and organizer for other Nazi-Muslim military divisions in Nazi-occupied areas of Europe with Muslim populations. He conducted a series of radio broadcasts from Nazi Germany, which were transmitted to the Arab world, and which included some of the most blood-curdling anti-Jewish statements and propaganda in history. Al-Husseini should be viewed as on par with any one of the most infamous Nazi villains and was in many respects far worse. This shocking story begs to be told and retold.

After the war, and after Yugoslavia attempted to indict him as a war criminal for crimes against humanity, al-Husseini fled to Cairo, where he remained as a guest of Egypt's King Farouk and one of his many protégés, General Gamel Abdel Nasser. Al-Husseini was received with fanfare in Cairo, where he remained headquartered for the rest of his infamous career. From Cairo, he devoted his considerable energy toward the destruction of the State of Israel, the poisoning of any vestiges of peace between Israel and the Arab states, and the destruction of the remaining Jewish communities in the Arab world. He would help Nazi war criminals settle in the Arab world through what is known as Operation Odessa. He would further encourage his followers to seize power in Arab capitals and to establish National Socialist–style governments.

There were three important phases in al-Husseini's career. The first phase covers the period from 1920, when he inspired the first pogrom against the Jewish settlers in Palestine, to 1937, when he met with the Nazi Adolf Eichmann in Palestine and concomitantly assumed a greater degree of influence in the Arab world at large. The second phase covers the period from the 1937 Eichmann meeting, through his involvement in the Nazi-inspired Iraq coup, and on to his activities in Nazi Germany until the end of the war in 1945. The third phase covers his activities from the end of the war to his death in Beirut in 1974.

My contention is that muftism, a term that has been used to describe the poisonous and fanatic legacy of Amin al-Husseini, the grand mufti of Jerusalem, continues to maintain a firm grip on the Arab and Islamic mind and soul today, much to the detriment of the Muslim peoples who are forced to live under its stultifying and regressive socialistic jack-boot regimes, to the detriment of any possibility of peace between Israel and the Arabs, and to the detriment of peace between the Muslim and non-Muslim worlds. Much unnecessary death, pain, and suffering has been caused and will no doubt continue to be caused by al-Husseini's evil legacy.

After the defeat of Hitler in 1945, the Soviet Union and the apparatus of the international left, along with the detritus of the Nazi network, largely filled the power vacuum in the Arab Middle East. In the Cold War years, the international left, operating under the tutelage of the Soviet Union, has been the primary booster in the Middle East of the poisonous legacy of al-Husseini, a legacy of terrorism and fanatic Islam. While Europe was largely denazified after the war by the victorious Allies, Islamo-fascism has remained virtually unchecked as a political, philosophical, and spiritual force. Arab peoples continue to groan under Nazi-Muslim oppressive regimes and al-Husseini-influenced pan-Islamists continue to promote imperialism and hatred for those who refuse to submit to their ironfisted will. The legacy of al-Husseini has been one of perpetual war against non-Islamic minorities, non-Islamic nations, and non-Islamic peoples.

Al-Husseini's tireless and single-mindedly fanatical career contributed greatly to a regressive trend in the Arab and Islamic world. Progressive forward-thinking Arabs, who sought freedom-oriented societies, were top-

Great Britain's Division of the Mandated Area. 1921-1923

pled from positions of influence, driven out of public life or into exile, or in many cases murdered by the thuggish and radical philosophical followers of al-Husseini. His inheritance is a form of Islamo-fascism that continues to metastasize across the Islamic world, and the threat that this malevolent movement poses to the non-Muslim world will continue to grow as long as it remains unchallenged.

Al-Husseini's political and philosophical offspring continue to be animated by an Islamo-fascism that is virtually identical to that which was advocated by al-Husseini as he pontificated from his Nazi perch in Berlin during the war. It is incumbent upon those of us who admire freedom, peace, and genuine human progress to examine the career of this man, Haj Amin al-Husseini, the grand mufti of Jerusalem, as a means of understanding the present crisis in the Arab and Islamic world and the cruel enemy that now confronts us. To suggest that such an examination is somehow anti-Arab is ludicrous, and as dangerous as a suggestion that an examination of Hitler and Nazism is somehow anti-German. If nothing else, the destructive and violent career of al-Husseini serves as a testament to the degree in which one man can influence and change the course of history.

Emir Faisal and
the Missed Opportunity

The relationship between the Arabs and the Jews was by no means always harmonious over the centuries and was certainly unbalanced in that Jews, as well as Christians living in the Arab world, were customarily treated as *dhimmis*, or second-class citizens, with all the deprivations and humiliations that this implies. Nevertheless, the relationship between the Arabs and the Jews was relatively tolerable over the many centuries preceding the First World War. In fact, Jews living in the Arab and Islamic world experienced far less persecution than did the indigenous Christians who were forced to endure what can only be described as a slow motion, low-tech Holocaust that stretched over millennia.

A systematic murder campaign against the indigenous Christian population of the Middle East, one that would also include theft, persecution, forced conversions, and ethnic cleansing, would reach a climax of ferocity when the Ottoman Turks committed mass genocide against the Armenian Christians in the early twentieth century. The Turks followed up this monstrous program with the virtual annihilation of the ancient and indigenous Greek Christian populations of Asia Minor in the early 1920s. The brutal anti-Christian campaigns continue in parts of the Arab and Islamic world today and include the slaughter of Christians in southern Sudan, Lebanon, Cyprus, Pakistan, the Philippines, and East Timor, to name a few hot spots.

The emergence of modern Zionism as a political and organic movement, one that is also deeply rooted in the Torah, and one that is integral to the Jewish faith, is traceable to the French Emperor Napoleon Bonaparte's promise to establish a Jewish state in Palestine at the turn of the nineteenth century. Backing his words with action, Napoleon attempted to establish a Jewish Sanhedrin in Paris in the early 1800s and contributed greatly to the emancipation of the Jews of Europe. In 1798, Napoleon, leading a French expeditionary force, invaded and occupied Turkish-controlled Egypt. The French would remain in Egypt for three years.

The French occupation of Egypt in 1798 looms large in Arab history and was considered by Arabs to represent a pivotal and humiliating defeat of what had been up until that time a dominant and seemingly invincible Ottoman Turkey. The French incursion was a benchmark in terms of introducing modernity and democratic ideas into the region. From this point forward, the Ottoman Empire would precipitously decline at a time when Europe was ascendant. Due to subsequent European and Western acquiescence, however, along with the twentieth-century influence of first European-based Nazism and then European-based communism, the tide is now showing signs of turning toward Islam, and Europe and the West are now in danger of retreat in the face of an ascendant and radicalized Islamic movement. This situation certainly could, and probably will, change overnight, if and when the sleeping giant of the Western democracies is roused out of its state of somnambulance.

Zionism is a recurring theme in Jewish history that goes back to the patriarchs of the ancient days. Every generation from that time to the present has borne witness to a continuous Jewish presence in the land between the Jordan River and the Mediterranean Sea. Each generation has produced its Jewish pilgrims, adventurers, scholars, mystics, and travelers who have made their way to the Promised Land. Never once, from ancient times to the present, has there not been a Jewish presence in the land of Israel.

The modest Zionist aspirations in the Middle East were tolerated both in the region later called Palestine and by the Arabs in general in the nineteenth century during the waning years of Ottoman control. Egypt itself would subsequently fall under British influence after the departure of the French. The nineteenth century Yishuv, or Jewish community of Palestine, traced its ancestry directly back to Roman and pre-Roman times and, starting in the early nineteenth century, began to experience a more steady infusion of Jewish settlers as immigrants, often fleeing persecution elsewhere, made their way into the region. This was an entirely organic and spontaneous development.

In the early and mid-nineteenth century the Jewish residents of the region, both indigenous and immigrant, began to step outside of the safe walled cities, where traditionally the Jewish population resided, and to form settlements nearby and in the countryside. By the mid-nineteenth century, Jewish enclaves and villages were developing throughout the region.

Jewish immigration into Palestine began to noticeably pick up in the mid-nineteenth century. This resulted in the development of the first modern agricultural villages, as well as the first kibbutzim. Persecution and pogroms against the Jews of Eastern Europe concurrently began increasing in this period, culminating in an 1881 anti-Semitic edict from the Russian Czar Alexander II. The edict caused dislocations, forced evacuations, and slaughter. The most famous and bloody example was the pogrom in Kishniev, Russia, in 1903. This pogrom made international headlines and was condemned by American President Theodore

Theodor Herzl

Roosevelt. These persecutions dramatically increased Jewish immigration into Palestine. This late-nineteenth century wave of Jewish immigration is known in Israel today as the second aliyah.

The Zionist movement also received a significant international boost and European and American recognition as a political movement in 1897, when the first World Zionist Congress, chaired by the liberal Hungarian Jewish journalist Theodor Herzl, was convened in Basel, Switzerland. This event marked the birth of the modern Zionist movement.

Nineteenth-century Palestine was a poor and sparsely populated for-gotten corner of the Ottoman Turkish vilayet of Syria. To this day, many Syrians view the region as an integral part of a greater Syria. This claim springs from the fact that Syria more or less controlled the Palestine area while themselves under Turkish auspices for over four centuries. The word Palestine was assigned to the region by the Roman Emperor Hadrian, who derived it from the name of the ancient Jewish nemesis, the Philistines. Hadrian had defeated the Jewish rebels, led by Bar Kochba, in 138–140 CE, and sought to eradicate any memory of the Jewish people.

Hadrian mocked the defeated Jews by renaming the country Palestine, and in this same spirit, he renamed Jerusalem Aelia Capitalina and set up a shrine to Zeus on top of the ruins of the Jewish temple. The word Palestine is unlike any word in the Arabic language and, in fact, the letter "P" doesn't exist in Arabic. It was the Europeans, particularly the British, who were responsible for re-introducing the ancient Roman name Palestine in the formal sense. When the British established their post–World War I mandate, they called the southern portion of the Ottoman province of Syria "Palestine" while the French retained the name Syria for the northern portion, which they assumed control over after the bor-der was drawn following the Sykes-Picot agreement. The terms Palestine and Palestinian were actually used to describe Zionist Jewish settlers as opposed to the Arabs in the region. It was the Jewish residents, not the Arabs, who called themselves Palestinian in those decades.

The pan-Islamists of today, influenced by the legacy of the grand mufti of Jerusalem, claim that the Palestinian Arabs were fully settled and indigenous to this region, but this is contrary to all existing evi-dence and makes no sense. How could a massive immigration of peoples from Europe occur in a heavily populated land? The fact of the matter is that the land had been laid waste by the Mongol invaders centuries earlier and had never been rebuilt or resettled by the Turks who had subsequently re-conquered the area from the Mongols. A few elite Arab families, al-Husseini's among them, served as administrators for the Turks and collected taxes and rents for absentee landlords who con-trolled most of the area.

No less a figure than the great American novelist and journalist Mark Twain, in his travelogue *Innocents Abroad*, published in 1867, described the region known as Palestine as a "desolate country whose soil is rich enough, but is given over wholly to weeds—a silent mournful expanse. A desolation is here that not even imagination can grace with the pomp of life and action. . . .We never saw a human being on the whole route . . . .There was hardly a tree or a shrub anywhere. Even the olive and the cactus, those fast friends of a worthless soil, had almost deserted the country."

The truth of the matter is that Arabs also began to immigrate en masse into this sparsely populated region known as Palestine during the late nineteenth century. They began settling there during the same period as the Jews, and their immigration was largely motivated by a desire to benefit from the many economic benefits the European Jews were introducing into the region. The Zionist settlers were developing a modern democratic society in every sense, and that society naturally led to some friction and tensions with some of the more traditionalist elements of Islamic society in general.

A basic tenet of traditional Islamic custom is that the Prophet Mohammed must be imitated in all possible respects by his followers, including manner of dress, diet, and other mannerisms. Naturally, there was a resulting hostility from some quarters toward the Europeanized Jews with their modern and secular ways and the possibility that these ways might influence the Arabs. This same hostility toward the Western influence contributed to the development of reactionary Islamic sects such as the Muslim Brotherhood, the Wahabis in Arabia, and later Hamas, Islamic Jihad, and others.

A progressive Arab view toward the Western democracies and toward Zionism existed during the late nineteenth and early twentieth centuries. This view was held by the Emir Faisal ibn Hussein and by many enlightened and forward-thinking Arabs. I was astonished to discover, given the acrimony of today, that many Arabs during this period recognized the legitimate claims of Jews to Palestine. It was understood that recognition of a Jewish national home by the Arabs would coincide with a guarantee of Arab rights within the Jewish state and Islamic control of the holy sites. Faisal insisted that such recognition would have to coincide with the achievement of sovereignty by the Arab nations.

Emir Faisal, of the Bedouin Hashemite clan, which traced its ancestry back to the Prophet Mohammed himself, was considered to be the recognized head of the entire emerging Arab world at the end of World War I and was the officially accredited head of the Arab delegation to the Paris Peace Conference held at the conclusion of World War I. Faisal's brother Abdallah, later king of the eastern sector of Palestine known as Transjordan, would be the first Arab leader to meet with Dr. Chaim Weizmann. Yusuf Diya al-Khalidi, an Ottoman official who corresponded with Theodor Herzl, wrote to Herzl, "The idea itself (Zionism) is natural, fine, and just. Who can challenge the rights of the Jews in Palestine? . . . Historically it is really your country." (*Jerusalem Quarterly*, no. 41, Winter 1987).

Emir Faisal's party at Versailles, during the Paris Peace Conference of 1919. At the center, from left to right: Rustum Haidar, Nuri as-Said, Prince Faisal, Captain Pisani (behind Faisal), T.E. Lawrence, Faisal's slave (name unknown), Captain Hassan Khadri

On January 3, 1919, in London, Emir Faisal ibn Hussein, along with Dr. Chaim Weizmann, head of the Zionist Organization and Faisal's diplomatic counterpart as the officially accredited head of the Zionist delegation to the Paris Peace Conference, signed a treaty known as the Faisal-Weizmann Agreement. I would argue that this agreement constitutes a full recognition of a Jewish Palestine, renamed Israel at the time of independence from Britain, by the Arab nations and peoples and constitutes a firm and definable precedent in international law. The preamble to the agreement is a perfect and sublime illustration of the progressive and enlightened view of the many fair-minded Arabs at the time and since. The agreement makes eloquent reference to "the racial kinship and ancient bonds existing between the Arabs and the Jewish people" and refers to "the closest possible collaboration in the development of the Arab State and Palestine [Israel]" (*Appendix C*).

Article I of the agreement constitutes an explicit recognition of Palestine (Israel) by the Arabs with a call for "Arab and Jewish duly accredited agents" to be "established and maintained in their respective territories." Article II calls for a commission to define permanent boundaries between the Arab states and Palestine (Israel). An argument could be made that this clause was fulfilled in July 1922 when, under the auspices of Winston Churchill, acting as colonial secretary of Great Britain, the League of Nations–created British Mandate of Palestine was divided along the Jordan River into an eastern Arab sector, which was called Transjordan, or the land west of the Jordan River, and a western Jewish sector, which was called cis-Jordan or the land east of the Jordan River. Upon independence in 1948, Transjordan became the Kingdom of Jordan and cis-Jordan became the State of Israel. At the time of the partition of the British Mandate of Palestine in 1922, it was understood that Transjordan would be Arab Palestine and, as such, off-limits to Jewish immigration.

Nineteen twenty-two was the year that witnessed the first partition of Palestine into a Jewish and an Arab sector. This would be followed by many other attempts to partition the small Jewish sector of Palestine into Jewish and Arab sectors. In 1947, for example, the Jews accepted a United Nations resolution to divide Western Palestine into a Jewish and an Arab state in exchange for international recognition of Jewish sovereignty. The 1947 U.N.-sponsored partition proposal, embodied in U.N. Resolution 181, would have left the Jewish sector confined to a couple of noncontiguous gerrymandered enclaves and would have, at the same time, created a substantial and independent Arab Palestinian state west of the Jordan River. U.N. Resolution 181 was rejected by the Arabs with al-Husseini himself playing a considerable role in that rejection. It is entirely fair to state that in the right environment, yet another commission, acting in the spirit of the historic Faisal-Weizmann Agreement, could very well once again be established as a means of defining permanent and secure borders between the Arab nations and Palestine (Israel).

Article III formally recognized the Balfour Declaration in which "His Majesty's Government [Britain] views with favor the establishment in Palestine of a national home for the Jewish people." The Balfour Declaration, authored by British Lord Arthur Balfour, a British Christian Zionist, was the first step toward an international recognition of a

Jewish Palestine and the recognition stated in the Balfour Declaration extended, by the signing of the Faisal-Weizmann Agreement, to the entire Arab world. Article IV, astonishing in light of the subsequent Arab-Jewish conflict, actually encourages Jewish immigration into Palestine as long as "the Arab peasant and tenant farmers shall be protected in their rights, and shall be assisted in forwarding their economic development."

Article V constitutes a declaration of freedom of religion in Palestine and, by inference, in all of the Arab nations as well. Article VI insists that "Mohammedan Holy Places shall be under Mohammedan control" in Palestine, which goes a long way toward explaining why Israel has left the Temple Mount in Jerusalem and other Islamic holy sites under the control of Islamic authorities after the 1967 Six-Day War.

Article VII is most interesting in that it calls for "the Zionist Organization" to send a commission to both Palestine and to the Arab states to scope out various possibilities for economic development. Clearly, the informed view in the Arab world at the time was that a sovereign Jewish Palestine would play a significant role in assisting the emerging Arab states toward economic development and thus further a trend toward Arab self-determination and economic prosperity. In a sense, the fact that the Arabs ignored this aspect of the agreement is saddest of all. The only caveat in the agreement is that Arab sovereignty must be achieved and recognized or the agreement would be rendered null and void. Arab sovereignty in twenty-two Arab states has, of course, been a long-established and an unchallenged fact for many decades. The idea at the core of the Faisal-Weizmann Agreement was that the

1918. Emir Faisal I and Chaim Weizmann (left, also wearing Arab outfit as a sign of friendship)

Arabs and the Jews would achieve sovereignty together, and would work together in a spirit of harmony and cooperation toward the benefit of each respective nation.

There was a fascinating exchange of letters during this period between Emir Faisal and Professor Felix Frankfurter, at the time the dean of Harvard Law School and an influential American Jewish leader who would later be appointed to the Supreme Court by President Franklin D. Roosevelt, the so-called Faisal-Frankfurter Correspondence. In one of his letters to Felix Frankfurter, Faisal wrote, " . . .We feel that the Arabs and Jews are cousins in race, having suffered similar oppressions at the hands of powers stronger than themselves, and by a happy coincidence have been able to take the first step toward the attainment of their national ideals together."

This truly amazing and enlightened view toward Jews and Israel is virtually alien in today's Arab world. It is particularly striking that Faisal and Weizmann viewed both peoples and nations as advancing together and lending mutual assistance toward the mutual realization of their respective national, political, and cultural rights. It is extraordinary that Faisal understood the potential benefits that such a partnership could offer the emerging Arab states. Faisal spoke for many Arabs in his day when he asserted in his letters to Felix Frankfurter, "We Arabs, especially the educated among us, look with the deepest sympathy on the Zionist movement."

Faisal reasserted his acceptance of the Faisal-Weizmann Agreement in his letters to Felix Frankfurter when he stated that he was "fully acquainted with the proposals submitted yesterday by the Zionist Organization to the Peace Conference and we regard them as moderate and proper." And so they were then and so they remain today. It should be shouted from the rooftops that, indeed, Jewish claims in Palestine then and now, both in accordance with the Torah and in the spirit of the modern Zionist movement, are and have always been "moderate and proper."

Zionism was, is, and shall forever remain a national movement for a sovereign Jewish homeland in Palestine, nothing more and nothing less. It should be pointed out that the proposed Jewish Palestine that Faisal was referring to in the Faisal-Weizmann Agreement actually included both banks of the Jordan, which today constitute the nations of Israel and Jordan. Proper and appropriate adjustments were made a couple of years after the signing of the Faisal-Weizmann Agreement dividing Palestine into Arab and Jewish sectors, adjustments that were fully conceded to by the Zionists. Both Faisal and Weizmann represented a nationalist point of view in the best meaning of the term, which was that both supported the concept of free and sovereign democratic republics. Al-Husseini, on the other hand, like Hitler, his collaborator, was an imperialist and an internationalist.

The fact of the matter, a fact that is rarely mentioned in Islamic circles today, is that Faisal, by recognizing a Jewish state in Palestine, was actually acting very much in accord with the written Koran as well as within certain understandings of traditional Islamic teachings and thought. Faisal was a traditionalist as well as a modern Muslim in the best meaning of the term. Regarding the establishment of a Jewish state in Palestine, the Koran is in complete conformity with the Torah when it says:

> . . .the words of Moses to his people. He said: "Remember, my people, the favors, which Allah has bestowed upon you . . . . Enter, my people, the holy land which Allah has assigned for you" (Sura V).

> . . . when the promise of the hereafter cometh to pass (at Judgment Day) we shall bring you as a crowd gathered out of various nations" (Sura XVII: 104).

Faisal stated the situation as he saw it in plain and unvarnished terms when he wrote the letters to Felix Frankfurter in which he stated "the Jewish movement is national and not imperialist; our movement is national and not imperialist; and there is room in Syria for us both. Indeed, I think that neither can be a real success without the other." Zionism, contrary to conspiracy theories that would later be penned by Adolf Hitler in *Mein Kampf* and then disseminated in the Arab world by al-Husseini, was not at all imperialist, but was rather a modest movement striving toward a national self-determination that envisioned a sovereign Jewish state existing within secure borders for its own sake and living peacefully with its Arab neighbors.

Astonishingly, Faisal went on in his correspondence with Frankfurter to assert that "we will do our best, in so far as we are concerned, to help them [the Jewish settlers] through. We will wish the Jews a most hearty welcome home." Faisal wrote, "Dr. Weizmann has been a great helper of our cause, and I hope the Arabs may soon be in a position to make the Jews welcome in return for their kindness. We are working together on a reformed and revived Near East, and our two movements complete one another."

Faisal's hope was that the newly emerging Arab states would be nationalist rather than imperialist and, as such, the Arab nations would take their rightful place alongside the other nations of the world that were emerging and achieving sovereignty in the post–World War I period. Faisal very much wanted his people to achieve all of the benefits and blessings of full political, economic, and cultural rights. He seemed to have grasped concepts such as democracy, limited government, and individual rights, ideas that were taking hold in this period and that were widely known to have been discussed by the participants at the Paris Peace Conference.

In the decades following the signing of the Faisal-Weizmann Agreement, al-Husseini led a regressive movement away from the spirit of Faisal-Weizmann as he gave voice and substance to tendencies within Islam that favored autocracy and imperialism. Al-Husseini was not alone and the Middle East didn't exist in a vacuum, as al-Husseini's contemporaries, Lenin, Stalin, and Hitler, were working the same side of the street in Europe.

Today, those same tendencies subject Arabs to autocracy and have led to aggressive and imperialistic wars against non-Muslim nations on the frontiers of the Islamic world. This aggression has not only targeted Israel, but has also targeted Christians in Lebanon and Egypt, Cyprus, Southern Sudan, Nigeria, India, the Philippines, East Timor, the African rim, Russia, China, and elsewhere. Osama bin Laden, the Taliban, Saddam Hussein, Hizbollah, Hamas, and Al Qaeda represent a modern embodiment of these tendencies. While Europe was denazified after World War II, and while the Soviet evil empire has collapsed, these tendencies continue to run rampant in the Middle East.

Faisal was not unaware of the potential difficulties that lay ahead. He stated to Frankfurter, "People less informed and less reasonable than our leaders and yours, ignoring the need for co-operation of the Arabs and Zionists, have been trying to exploit the local difficulties that must necessarily arise in Palestine in the early stages of our movement. Some of them have, I am afraid, misrepresented your aims to the Arab peasantry and our aims to the Jewish peasantry with the result that interested parties have been able to make capital out of what they call our differences." Certainly al-Husseini would be known in the ensuing years to use his position and influence in Palestine to spread inflammatory rumors among the Arabs in order to incite enmity toward the Jews.

The letter to Frankfurter finishes with a simple plea, the eloquence and magnanimity of which speaks for itself. " . . . I look forward, and my people with me look forward, to a future in which we will help you and you will help us, so that the countries in which we are mutually interested may once again take their places in the community of civilized people of the world."

The Emir Faisal, whose credentials as an Arab nationalist were well known, became king of Syria in 1920, but he was quickly removed from office by the French after a little over a year. In 1921, with British assistance, Faisal became king of the semi-autonomous British Mandatory Iraq, where he remained king until his death in 1933. Faisal's son and heir was Ghazi bin Faisal, who, unlike his father, proved to be more oriented toward a pan-Arab and anti-British stance. Ghazi  remained king until his death in 1939 and was succeeded by his three-year-old son Faisal bin Ghazi, known as Faisal II. While Faisal II inherited the kingdom, his uncle, Emir Abd al-Ilah, would act as the controlling regent until 1953, when Faisal II came of age. The Hashemite dynasty would last until July 14, 1958, when an officers' coup led by General Abdul Karim Kassem seized the government and assassinated both Emir al-Ilah and the twenty-two-year-old Faisal II.

Iraq was an entirely artificial nation created by British mapmakers and crafted out of the remains of the post–World War I Ottoman Empire. The European powers cobbled together three entirely different and distinct Ottoman Turkish vilayets to create Iraq. For approximately four hundred years, the Ottoman Turks had ruled over these

Associated Press—The captured former Iraqi leader is shown in Baghdad in this image from television.

lands and had viewed these three Mesopotamian vilayets as little more than a frontier and battleground between themselves and Iran. The Kurds are in the north, the Sunnis are in the region centered on Baghdad, and the Shiites are in the south. Each of the three groups has its own distinct and separate culture, as well as a history of animosity toward the other. Additionally, the Turks remained interested in reoccupying the northern region centered on the oil city of Mosul after the establishment of a British Protectorate. This situation essentially remains the same to this day and is the source of the ongoing conflict and instability within Iraq.

Given the hand that he was dealt in Iraq, King Faisal was an amazingly successful leader who contributed to crafting and furthering the interests of a modern state. With British help, King Faisal established democratic institutions, created the setting for the emergence of a private sector, and helped to develop a modern infrastructure. Faisal viewed the British as providers of temporary and transitional assistance in terms of helping Iraq develop into a modern and fully sovereign state. Much of the work of this enlightened ruler would be eroded and undone in the ensuing decades by the next generation of weaker Hashemite kings, the introduction of radical pan-Arabism in the 1930s, and by al-Husseini, who operated in Baghdad as the acknowledged mastermind behind a pro-Nazi generals' coup in 1941.

Al-Husseini, an agent of the Third Reich, was welcomed with great fanfare into Baghdad in 1941. His entry onto the scene marked a major shift in Iraqi politics. Thus al-Husseini contributed toward the introduction of Nazism into Iraq and the result was a legacy of totalitarian socialistic governments and the persecution of the Jewish minority. The first significant pogrom against the ancient and indigenous Iraqi Jews, known by the Sephardic Jews as the Farhud, occurred in the immediate aftermath of the al-Husseini inspired coup. The final nail was hammered into the Iraqi Jewish coffin in 1951-1952 when 250,000 Jews, virtually the entire remaining Jewish community in Iraq, were driven out of the country with little more than the shirts on their backs following several highly visible murders of Jews. The insidious injection of al-Husseini and his philosophy into Iraqi politics in 1941 would set the stage for the eventual emergence of the monstrous beast, al-Husseini disciple, and mass murderer Saddam Hussein.

The Mufti Makes His Grand Debut

Haj Amin al-Husseini was born in Jerusalem around 1895, at a time when Palestine was still a subsector of the Ottoman Turkish vilayet of Syria. He came from a wealthy and prominent Jerusalem Arab clan. His grandfather Mustapha and his half-brother Kemal would precede him as mufti of Jerusalem. Members of his family had served the Ottoman Turks as civil servants for generations preceding the arrival of the British in 1918. The prefix "Haj" signifies that al-Husseini had completed the Islamic obligation of performing a pilgrimage, or hajj, to Mecca, which he performed with his mother in 1913.

Al-Husseini attended the prestigious Al-Azhar University in Cairo for about a year, where he studied Islamic law. Al-Azhar was known as a hotbed of radical politics and fundamentalist Islam. At Al-Azhar, al-Husseini was no doubt exposed to the concept that Islamic law, or sharia, ought to be applied as the governing principle, and that religious war, or jihad, ought to be launched against those who fail to submit.

In 1914, at the outbreak of World War I, Ottoman Turkey joined the Central powers and al-Husseini joined the Ottoman army, where he received a commission as an artillery officer. Al-Husseini was stationed with the Forty-seventh brigade, which was based in the predominantly

Greek Christian city of Smyrna. The brigade also served in bases near the Black Sea. The Ottomans were allied with Germany, Austria-Hungary, and Bulgaria.

There is no hard evidence that al-Husseini participated in the Turkish genocide against the indigenous Armenian Christians. There is, however, massive and well-documented evidence of the Turkish program of genocide, which caused the deaths of millions of Armenians. The genocide was in full swing during al-Husseini's years of service and he was stationed in areas where it would have been carried out. The genocide was well known in Turkey, especially within the Ottoman military, which was charged with carrying it out.

An estimated one and a half million Armenians were slaughtered and starved to death by the Ottomans in those years alone. It is reasonable to assume that al-Husseini had at least some knowledge of, if not a level of direct participation in, this first holocaust of the twentieth century. His involvement is quite plausible, especially in light of his subsequent direct and intimate participation in the Nazi Holocaust against the Jews several decades later.

In November of 1916, al-Husseini left the Turkish Army under the guise of a disability, receiving a three-month leave. He returned to Jerusalem where he remained on leave until the end of the war. The Allied powers defeated the Turks and the British occupied the region then known as southern Syria in 1918. The British established a military administration on both banks of the Jordan River in a region that they chose to call Palestine.

At the end of the First World War, the victorious Allied powers divided Ottoman Syria between Great Britain and France in what is known as the Sykes-Picot agreement. According to all recorded accounts concerning al-Husseini, he was in those years and throughout his life an ardent and, indeed, a fanatical follower of the imperial pan-Arab principle of the caliphate and, as such, he opposed the division of Syria. Al-Husseini's pan-Arab convictions were most likely enhanced during his brief tenure at Al-Azhar in Cairo. It should also be noted that during the period of al-Husseini's youth and formative years, Ottoman Turkey, while drawing its last gasps of glory after having borne the mantle of militant Islam for centuries, nevertheless remained a great embodiment of Muslim imperial aspirations.

Al-Husseini would prove to be a bridge figure in terms of catapulting

Amin al-Husseini as an officer of the Ottoman Empire—1915

the old and imperialist ideas of Islam and Ottoman Turkey into modern times, ideas that were opposed by the more enlightened Arabs at the time. Pan-Arabism is a philosophy that calls for a solitary and united Arab nation, one that would exist at the center of a concentric circle with a greater Islamic nation making up the next ring, the great caliphate, made up of the entire and united Arab and Muslim world. This utopian entity, in turn, was commanded to engage in a perpetual jihad, or holy war, against the non-submitting world until the utopian dar el-Islam, or the world utterly controlled by Islam, was achieved.

The religious idea used to justify the imperialistic and radical element within Islam is that a world living under the forceful hand of the scimitar would represent a physical manifestation of the spiritual ideal, which is the unity and oneness of Allah. The united Arab inner core, united both spiritually and by the earthly force of arms, is called in Arabic the *ummah* or, loosely translated, the "Motherland." The *ummah*, according to an aspect of Islamic tradition, is ruled by a caliph, who would theoretically inherit his mantle of earthly authority from the Prophet Mohammed himself in a manner that is not entirely unlike the concept undergirding the Roman Catholic pontiff, who, according to Roman Catholic tradition, is the earthly inheritor of the ministry of Jesus Christ.

The difference, in today's terms, between the Catholic concept of the pontiff and the Islamic concept of the caliph, however, is that the caliph, besides being a spiritual and religious leader, is also a political and military ruler who is empowered to forcibly implement sharia, or Islamic law, at the tip of the scimitar. The caliph, according to Koranic and other Islamic texts, is commanded to lead the bloody charge in a perpetual jihad, or holy war, against the portion of the world that refuses to submit to Islam. In its literal translation, the very word Islam means "submission to Allah." The military and conquering aspect of the Islamic faith is the aspect that was embraced by al-Husseini and is presently embraced by Osama bin Laden, the hijackers who destroyed the twin towers in New York City on September 11, 2001, the Taliban, Hamas, and the rest of the international Islamic terror apparatus.

The mystical and utopian state of Dar el-Islam is achieved when the entire world submits to Islam, according to certain passages found in traditional Islamic texts. Such submission by all of the peoples of the world is supposed to represent the fulfillment of the prophesies of Mohammed and is supposed to manifest the physical proof of the existence and majesty of Allah on earth. All of humanity, living in the utopian Dar el-Islam, would then be expected to completely submit itself to sharia, or Islamic law.

Non-Muslims, or *dhimmis*, were tolerated in the Islamic world as long as they submitted to Islamic control and maintained themselves in a second-class status. Special laws applied to *dhimmis*, including their payment of a special yearly tax, or *jizya*, which entitled them to live for another year as a non-Muslim. Al-Husseini held to the principle that Jews living in Palestine before a certain date would be allowed to remain as *dhimmis* with no rights. Al-Husseini also expressed the belief that any land conquered by Muslims, at any time in history, would be a part of the *waqf*, or the holy trust, to be controlled forever by Muslims.

During the 1929 Arab pogrom against the Jewish Yishuv, a pogrom in which the entire indigenous Jewish community of Hebron was wiped out, al-Husseini expressed, as justification for his instigation of the attacks, that he was fearful over the prospect that Palestine might become another Andalusia. This is the Islamic name for Moorish Spain, which was conquered by the Catholic kingdom of Castile in the fifteenth century.

For the pan-Arabist, the concept of jihad or holy war is interpreted to literally mean "bloody war," if all other means fail, against what is called the Dar al-Harb, or the "world of war," which constitutes that portion of the world that refuses all other entreaties to submit to Islamic rule. This concept goes to the heart of understanding the motive behind Islamic terror worldwide.

This particular Islamic worldview finds many parallels, of course, in the worldview of the modern European socialist movements such as Nazism, which called for the creation of a new social order controlled by the übermensch, and communism, which called for a socialist workers' world that is ruled by a "dictatorship of the proletariat." The idea of creating an earthly utopia by force—and there is no other way, since utopias are unnatural—is an enduring and animating idea, one that continues to plague human existence and one that is by no means unique to Islam.

Government is, de facto, a form of legalized force, and the earthly utopians view government as an agent of change and as an instrument toward achieving human salvation. Of course, the goals of all world order movements are, a priori, contrary to human nature, which naturally gravitates toward such concepts as individual liberty, freedom of thought and action, and a limited role for government. This is why all utopian world order movements in history, without exception, whether communist, Nazi, radical pan-Islamist, or other, resort to the force of arms and the annihilation of a real, perceived, or invented opposition to their controlling designs.

In the same way that al-Husseini represented the pan-Arab point of view, Adolf Hitler, whose career parallels and intersects with al-Husseini's, represented the pan-Germanic point of view. The pan-Arabist seeks a world empire based on his or her interpretation of the Islamic faith, with the Arab language and culture serving as the centerpiece. Likewise, the Nazi pan-Aryan sought a world empire with a mystical concept of the Germanic race serving as the centerpiece, as opposed to faith or language. The pan-Arabist believes that the Arab *ummah* must serve as the central governing authority over the less enlightened Islamic and non-Islamic world, while the Nazi pan-Ary-ans, believed that the German fatherland, including a union of all German-speaking and racially Aryan peoples, would have provided the central authority for the rest of Europe and the centerpiece for a new world order. While pan-Arabism is religious and socialist, Nazism is secular, socialist, and socially Darwinian.

The pan-Arab agenda, as promoted by al-Husseini, is made plain in the Palestinian National Covenant, which is a perfect repository of current pan-Arab thinking. Article I of the covenant states: "Palestine is the homeland of the Arab Palestinian people; it is an indivisible part of the Arab homeland, and the Palestinian people are an integral part of the Arab nation" (*Appendix I*). Note that Palestine is considered in the covenant to be an "indivisible" and "integral" part of the Arab home-land, or *ummah*, which presumably includes all regions of the world where Arabic is the majority language. This concept is, for all intents and purposes, identical to the Nazi concept of the Third Reich, in which the Nazis claimed for themselves the right to directly control all German-speaking peoples. In fact, World War II was really instigated by the Nazi insistence on uniting the German-speaking nations of Germany and Austria, and then controlling the German-speaking part of Czechoslovakia, called Sudetenland, and the German-speaking regions of Poland.

Amin al-Husseini carried his pan-Arab ideas into Palestine at a time when Emir Faisal, and many if not most Arabs, including most Palestinian Arabs, were proceeding both with the goals of the British Mandate, which were in support of a Jewish national home within mod-est and proper borders as called for in the Balfour Declaration of 1918 and the Faisal-Weizmann Agreement, and the attainment of national Arab sovereignty in the Arab lands recently liberated from Ottoman control. In the service of these goals, Emir Faisal would first become king of Syria in 1920, and than later become king of Iraq, where he ruled from 1921 to 1933. Al-Husseini resented the British Mandate in Palestine and hated the Jewish settlers, who numbered at about sixty thousand at the time of his return from Ottoman service, as opposed to about eight hundred thousand Muslims.

In the period 1917-1919, al-Husseini supported the return of the newly created Palestine to Syrian control. He worked with his friend and collaborator Arif al-Arif, the editor of a newspaper called *Suriyah al-Janubiyah* (Southern Syria), to further this principle. In 1919, al-Husseini attended a pan-Syrian congress, which was held in Damascus and where he supported Emir Faisal in his effort to become king of Syria. A brilliant organizer and agitator, the young al-Husseini began to organize a secretive Muslim youth group in Palestine with a strong militaristic component and he began to agitate against the British, the Zionists, and moderate Muslims.

To further his efforts, al-Husseini tapped into his considerable family wealth and utilized a growing network of personal and political contacts. His group was called al-Nadi al-Arabi (The Arab Club). It was established in 1919, and the youth group quickly took on the coloration of a quasi-military gang of thugs. The stated agenda of al-Nadi al-Arabi was to return Palestine to Syria, to expel the Zionists, and, as an ultimate article of faith, to contribute in the establishment of the *ummah*.

Al-Husseini was the instigator, along with his editor friend Arif al-Arif, of an attack on innocent Jews praying at the Western Wall in Jerusalem in March of 1920 in the days immediately following Passover. This bloody attack in Jerusalem, which led to attacks against Jews throughout Palestine, is known in Israel as "bloody Passover." A well-coordinated chain reaction to the initial attack against Jews led to Arab gangs attacking Jews in Jaffa, Rehovot, Petah Tikva, and other Jewish towns. A total of forty-seven Jews were killed and over 140 wounded in the first significant bloodshed in Palestine in hundreds of years.

The British authorities responded by refusing to intervene to protect the Jews and instead arrested several Jews, including American Zionist journalist Vladimir Jabotinsky, for trying to form a self-defense league. This slaughter and the subsequent rioting by Arabs, along with the British refusal to respond, provided the main catalyst for the creation by the Jews of the Hagana, or self-defense forces. It was this incident that led to the beginning of a parting of the ways between the two Palestinian communities, the Jews and the Arabs, and marked the formal launching of hostilities.

The British subsequently indicted al-Husseini for the incitement that led to the murders and riots. He was tried and convicted in absentia, and sentenced to ten years in prison. At the time of his indictment, al-Husseini had already jumped bail and had taken refuge in Syria. The British authorities pardoned him shortly after his conviction and he returned to Palestine, where he continued to develop his network of terrorists and to agitate in favor of a re-absorption of Palestine into Syria. The idea that Israel, Jordan, and Lebanon are a part of a greater Syria is an idea that continues to hold a great deal of currency in Syria today.

The Arabs of Palestine during this period held many divergent views regarding their identity and future. Those who tended toward the pan-Arab view were more likely to support a return to Syrian jurisdiction, Syria having controlled Palestine as a sub-province for approximately four hundred years under Ottoman auspices. Some Palestinian Arabs supported the idea of an Arab State within the artificial borders of the British Mandate of Palestine, borders that had been drawn up by the British, and some Palestinian Arabs supported cooperation and power sharing with the Zionists. Either way, the al-Husseini-inspired blood letting of 1920 inexorably set the two populations on a collision course.

It should be reiterated that al-Husseini was a lifetime advocate of the pan-Arab point of view, a view he expressed often and within various contexts in his long career. The general ambivalence of Arabs regarding an Arab-Palestinian identity continues to this day and finds expression in the Palestinian National Covenant, which is plainly a pan-Arab doctrine. The covenant calls for a Palestinian Arab entity to serve the purpose of destroying the Jewish state. The newly established Palestinian "state" would then, according to the covenant, serve as a stepping-stone toward the achievement of the pan-Arab and Islamic *ummah* (*Appendix I*).

The newly appointed civilian British High Commissioner Sir Herbert Samuel, himself a British Jew, pardoned al-Husseini shortly after he assumed his post in 1921, thus allowing him to return to Palestine. It should be noted that al-Husseini had at this point been convicted of inciting a terror campaign against Jewish settlers. He had also and simultaneously launched an internecine campaign of terror against the more moderate Palestinian Arabs who opposed him. This trend of terrorism against the more moderate Arabs and Muslims would subsequently spread, at the urging of al-Husseini and others, into the rest of the Arab and Islamic world, and the terror against moderate Arabs and Muslims continues to rage on to this day.

William Ziff, in his book *The Rape of Palestine*, comments on the significance of the appointment of al-Husseini as grand mufti of Jerusalem:

Implicated in the [1920] disturbances was a political adventurer named Haj Amin al-Husseini. Haj Amin was sentenced by a British court to fifteen years hard labor. Conveniently allowed to escape by the police, he was a fugitive in Syria. Shortly after, the British then allowed him to return to Palestine where, despite the opposition of the Muslim High Council who regarded him as a hoodlum, Haj Amin was appointed by the British High Commissioner as Grand Mufti of Jerusalem for life.

Before the appointment of al-Husseini as grand mufti by Sir Samuel, the Palestinian Arab leadership had traditionally voted for a new mufti, and Amin al-Husseini had come in a distant forth in this poll. One of the reasons al-Husseini was so thoroughly rejected for the position of mufti by the Arabs was that he was not considered to be a sheikh, which is to say that he was not viewed as having had a sufficient religious education, which is a requirement for the position. In addition, al-Husseini had already established a violent reputation in his dealings with rival Arabs, and this might have also played a role in their rejection of his candidacy. As mufti, al-Husseini would live up to that reputation by launching a bloody wave of terror and assassination against his Arab opponents.

Shortly after his appointment as grand mufti in March 1922, al-Husseini was also appointed by Sir Samuel to head the political

Supreme Muslim Council in Jerusalem. The Supreme Muslim Council had been set up by the British to provide political representation for the Palestinian Arabs. With both political and religious leadership positions in hand, al-Husseini was free to harass and drive out Arabs who favored a cooperative policy toward the Jewish settlers, and he staffed these organizations with like-minded fanatics. This was accomplished through threats and terror against moderates, methods that would be increasingly emulated throughout the Arab world as the influence and prestige of al-Husseini increased. On April 25, 1936, al-Husseini was also appointed to head the political and more radical Arab Higher Committee, a position that he held until the British deported him from Palestine on October 1, 1937.

The Supreme Muslim Council was dissolved in 1948 when the Arab Kingdom of Jordan occupied Jerusalem during Israel's War of

Independence and then later reconvened in Jerusalem after the June 1967 Six-Day War, when all of Jerusalem fell under Israeli control. Al-Husseini had used his authority as grand mufti and as head of the council in the 1920s and 1930s to issue fatwas against the British and the Jews. The present mufti of Jerusalem and head of the Supreme Muslim Council remains very much cut of the same cloth as his predecessor, al-Husseini. The present mufti, for example, has assumed a leading position as an outspoken denier of the Nazi Holocaust.

During the 2001 pilgrimage of Pope John Paul II to Jerusalem, the present grand mufti of Jerusalem, Sheikh Ikrima Sabri, stated of the Nazi Holocaust, "It's true, the number was less than six million and Israel is using this issue to get sympathy worldwide." Sabri also asserted, "It's not my problem. Muslims didn't do anything on this issue. It's the doing of Hitler who hated the Jews." Sabri is no doubt fully cognizant of the career of his predecessor as mufti, Amin al-Husseini, and his intimate relationship with Hitler, a topic that we will soon delve into.

Upon becoming grand mufti in 1921, al-Husseini declared a fatwa of jihad against the Zionists and simultaneously declared that all Muslims who maintained friendly relations with the Jews were to be considered as infidels, an enduring conviction in many quarters to this day. Al-Husseini also organized and launched the first modern Muslim fedayeen suicide squads in Palestine with the primary target of attack being moderate Palestinian Arabs who refused to cooperate. The cumulative result of al-Husseini's policies was the flight of moderate Arabs from Palestine in the ensuing decades, as dissent was squelched as al-Husseini consolidated his power. Al-Husseini also became known for employing the standard tactic of fomenting hatred of the Jews among the Arab population by spreading false rumors and other incitements.

From the time he became grand mufti of Jerusalem in 1921 until the pogroms and riots of 1929, al-Husseini further consolidated his grip over all of Arab Palestine. In the 1920s, besides holding the office of grand mufti, which was a religious office, and besides also heading the Supreme Muslim Council, which was a political office, al-Husseini also obtained control over the Arab charitable funds, known as the *waqf*, the court system, the offices of local muftis, and other religious institutions. He accomplished this with the full acquiescence and the tacit assistance of the British authorities in exchange for his promise to maintain the peace, a promise he tactically kept during this period of consolidation. In his ascension to power, al-Husseini received significant support from an element within the British Mandate Administration that was distinctly anti-Zionist.

While the centuries-old Ottoman Empire had maintained a long tradition of absolute rule by a sultan, nevertheless, the Ottoman style of government was to grant a degree of autonomy to the provinces and sub-sectors and to create a network of loyal civil servants, who would often come from the same clan and who would themselves be granted a considerable degree of autonomy. In this regard, the Ottomans allowed for the development of an informal system of checks and balances in the local and regional realms of religious, civil, judicial, and royal jurisdictions where families would maintain local fiefdoms and would often pass the baton on to succeeding generations. These divisions of governmental functions would further a system of competition between clans that would allow an administration in Istanbul to rule by the principal of divide and conquer. Al-Husseini's clan was one of those that had served the Ottoman authorities.

As grand mufti, al-Husseini broke with this tradition and moved toward the style of an absolute ruler in Palestine, a style that was simultaneously sweeping Europe in those years. Starting with the Bolshevik seizure of Russia in 1917, and followed by Mussolini and his march on Rome, European nations were increasingly embracing the authoritarian principle where all governmental power would reside in the hands of a single supreme commander. Al-Husseini replaced the traditional informal system of government in Palestine with a supreme command centered on his authoritarian personality. In this sense, along with his pronounced and well-articulated Jew hatred, he would prove to be an ideological soulmate of Hitler, his World War II political partner.

Like Hitler, al-Husseini demolished any opposition to his control, and like Hitler, al-Husseini insisted on one-man rule and total conformity to his view. Al-Husseini was a full and witting practitioner of what the Nazis called the *Führerprinzip*.

A major project of al-Husseini's in the 1920s was the raising of funds throughout the Arab world for the purpose of improving the Temple Mount, the site of the ancient Jewish temple known to Arabs as the al-Haram al-Sharif. The funds were specifically earmarked for the gold plating of the Dome of the Rock and improvements to the Al Aqsa Mosque in Jerusalem. Photos of Jerusalem before this time show a colorless and rather nondescript dome on top of the Temple Mount. These improvements served the practical purpose of enhancing the importance of Jerusalem in the Islamic world, which up until that point had been little more than an insignificant religious backwater. The fundraising also served to increase the prestige and influence of al-Husseini in the Arab and Islamic world as fundraisers from al-Husseini's Supreme Muslim Council traveled to major Muslim capitals looking for donations. Al-Husseini used these fundraising ambassadors to propagandize against the Zionists. This was accomplished with the use of false claims, such as that the Zionists were plotting to destroy the mosques on top of the Temple Mount in order to make way for the rebuilding of the Jewish Temple.

Temple Mount, Jerusalem

It should be acknowledged at this point that a growing number of Arabs living in Palestine during those years were frustrated over the increase in Jewish settlers. They were concerned about losing control over their ability to determine their own destiny. What was shaping up in Palestine in those years, and what has largely remained ever since, was a civil war between two different peoples, both with their own distinct language, religion, culture, and governing philosophy. While the comparison is certainly flawed, there are parallels to the situation in Palestine and the one that existed during the American Civil War of 1861-1865, when two different cultures and styles of government, that of the Union and that of the Confederacy, struggled for the future of America. The Confederacy, like the Arab movement in Palestine, was valiantly committed to a set of ideals that were compelling enough that young men were willing to fight and die to defend them.

General Ulysses S. Grant captured the Civil War struggle in his memoirs, a situation that was analogous, I would contend, to that of the struggle between the two Palestinian populations. In his memoir, Grant was reflecting on General Robert E. Lee's surrender of the Confederate Army of Northern Virginia at Appomattox on April 9, 1865, when he described his mood at the time: "I felt like anything rather than rejoicing at the downfall of a foe who had fought so long and valiantly, and had suffered so much for a cause, though that cause was, I believe, one of the worst for which a people ever fought, and one for which there was the least excuse. I do not question, however, the sincerity of the great mass of those who were opposed to us."

The Zionist cause was one that sought sovereignty for the Jewish people in the tiny speck of land between the Jordan River and the Mediterranean Sea, in a land that the Jewish people had maintained ties to going back to the ancient days. Al-Husseini's cause was, according to his many public utterances, the attainment of a vast and united Arab caliphate that would eventually set the stage for the utopian Dar el-Islam, or the world under Islam. At the time, the Arabs were in the process of obtaining sovereign national homelands in twenty-two vast, and in many cases, oil-rich states, while the Zionists sought a homeland in only one, the tiny land that the Almighty of the Bible has promised Abraham, Isaac, and Jacob. Al-Husseini represented an old and regressive strain contained within Islam, a strain that would have relegated all non-Muslims living in an Islamic state to *dhimmi* status, or second-class status, while the Zionists offered the Arabs of Palestine full citizenship and autonomy and left the Islamic holy sites under the control of the *wakf*, as stipulated by the Faisal-Weizmann Agreement.

Having said this, it should be pointed out that the conflict between the Arabs and the Zionist settlers was in many ways a reenactment of a theme that stretches back to the very beginning of civilization. There are countless examples in history of cultures and peoples who clash as a result of one group settling either near or within the region of another. Among the numerous historical examples of this phenomenon are the seventh-century Arab-Muslim conquest of the indigenous Christian countries of the Middle East and North Africa, the Anglo-Saxon settlement of Celtic Britain, the Scots-Irish settlement of Northern Ireland, the Dutch settlement of South Africa, the Spanish settlement of Central and South America, the Portuguese settlement of Brazil, and the British settlement of North America, Australia, and New Zealand.

The reaction of such an introduction of a new culture has often been violent on both sides. I will give an example of such a conflict in my own home state of Massachusetts. When the English colonists first settled in Boston and set up the Massachusetts Bay Colony, they maintained friendly relations with the native tribes, then under the rule of Chief Massasoit. At first, the colonists lived in relative harmony with their Native American neighbors. Then, upon the death of Massasoit, his son, Wampanoag Chief Metacom, known by his English name of

King Philip, became the head of the tribe and hatched a plot to completely annihilate the English settlements. Phillip hated the colonists because his brother, and several of his tribesmen, had been put to death after having been found guilty of murder by juries composed of colonists and natives, trials that were conducted in accordance with a treaty between the colony and the Native Americans.

Philip started a rumor among his fellow tribesmen, as well as among the surrounding New England tribes, that these trials were secretly fixed by the colonists. After five years of lobbying other tribes, King Philip organized and fielded a united native league of approximately three thousand warriors. What is known to history as King Philip's War began in June of 1675 with a massacre of colonists by the native league in the colonial village of Swansea. The violence and mayhem quickly spread throughout Massachusetts, with King Philip's forces, along with those of allied tribes, descending on colonial settlements and causing many wholesale slaughters. After many cruel massacres of colonists, involving the butchering of men, women, and children, the war ended as suddenly as it began when a trusted aide assassinated King Philip in August of 1676. As the native confederation collapsed in disarray, the colonial forces responded with a vigorous and decisive military force including a fearful slaughter of the natives.

One fundamental difference between the conflict that resulted in King Philip's War and the one that developed between the Zionist settlers and the Arabs is that Arab sovereignty and culture, unlike that of Native American sovereignty and culture, was not in any way threatened by the existence of a Jewish state in Palestine. The Arabs were already well on the road toward achieving sovereignty in twenty-one states at the time of the increase in Jewish settlement in Palestine. Unlike the English colonists arriving in the new world, the Jews had a well-known, long-standing, and universally accepted history in the area called Palestine and their claims were recognized by Islam as well, a recognition that is explicitly expressed in the Koran.

The Jewish settlers were willing to share sovereignty in the tiny land in exchange for peace and attempted to do so in many incidences documented in this book. Al-Husseini was an unyielding absolutist in that he maintained, throughout his long career, an intransigent insistence that the Jews had absolutely no rights in Palestine whatsoever. He rigidly refused to compromise on this position. My contention is that al-Husseini was driven by an imperialist vision fueled by aspects of Islam that were later enhanced by his embrace of Nazism, and that his motives were driven by a demonstrable and inveterate hatred for Jews. Al-Husseini further exacerbated and enshrined this hatred by working mightily to insure that the many Arab leaders and people who opposed his views were silenced.

Al-Husseini mixed religion, specifically the false claim that the Zionists plotted to destroy Muslim holy sites, with politics as a means of stirring up hatred against the Jews. In the Faisal-Weizmann Agreement, the Zionists promised to respect Muslim holy sites, and Israel continues to honor this commitment today, as, for example, the Temple Mount remains in Muslim hands. Passages in the Koran actually call for the establishment of Jewish sovereignty centered on Jerusalem. This portion of the Koran, while understood and respected by moderate and fair-minded Muslims at the time, was ignored by al-Husseini, who instead chose to emphasize Koranic passages that call for the slaughter of Jews who refuse to submit. While the Palestinian Arab cause had its merits, as did the Confederate cause in America, the Zionist cause, like the Union cause, was arguably the superior of the two.

The temporary peace of 1921-1929 was shattered when al-Husseini, after having delivered an incendiary speech at the al-Aqsa Mosque on August 23, 1929, instigated a riot that quickly spread throughout Palestine. One interesting and telling comment delivered by al-Husseini during that speech at al-Aqsa was the observation that Palestine might be lost to the *ummah* in the same way that Andalusia, which is the Arabic name for Iberia, was lost in the fifteenth century to the advancing forces of Catholic Spain. The underlying sentiment being expressed here was that any land occupied by Muslim forces was to be viewed as a personal and eternal possession of the *ummah* and as sacred. Any retreat in the Muslim great leap forward toward the pan-Islamic universe was viewed by al-Husseini as anathema, and indeed many Muslim clerics and intellectuals continue to bemoan the loss of Andalusia to this day.

On the day following al-Husseini's speech, a day that happened to fall on the Jewish Sabbath, a wholesale slaughter of sixty-seven Jews took place in the old and indigenous Palestinian Jewish community of Hebron. Six days later, on August 30, twenty Jews were massacred in the ancient Jewish city of Safad and much of that city's Jewish neighborhood was looted and burned. Al-Husseini instigated this pogrom of 1929, which resulted in the murders of one hundred and thirty-three Jews with over three hundred wounded.

The wholesale carnage against the Jews was triggered by the false and bizarre rumor circulated by al-Husseini that the Zionists had defiled local mosques, including al-Aqsa. In an orchestrated response to this preposterous lie, the call went out from al-Husseini supporters to the Arab masses to *"Itbakh al-Yahud!"* or "Slaughter the Jews!" al-Husseini would directly issue this call for genocide many times throughout his career, and this slogan remains a mainstay among his progeny to this day.

It should be noted that al-Husseini was not calling for the slaughter of the Zionists, but specifically for the slaughter of the Jews. Most of the Jews who were slaughtered in this particular bloodbath were indigenous Jews whose ancestors had lived in Palestine for centuries and who were not necessarily pro-Zionist. This further buttresses the claim that al-Husseini had embraced an anti-Jewish, as well as an anti-Zionist, stance, and that he had developed the tactic of using anti-Jewish conspiracy theories to whip up murderous mobs. Whether he was influenced in his actions by analogous events occurring simultaneously in pre-Nazi Germany is not known, but quite plausible.

After the slaughter of Hebron's Jews, photographs were disseminated of the slaughtered Jewish corpses with the claim that the dead were actually Arabs killed by Jews. This type of tactic is an example of the classic blood libel against the Jewish people, a tactic that finds its roots in medieval Europe, where the libelous claim was first lodged that the Jews had slaughtered Christian babies in order to bake Passover matzo. Lies of this nature would be used to whip mobs into a frenzy, and the predictable end result was usually a slaughter of Jews and a looting and robbing of the property of Jews.

Yasir Arafat employed this same type of blood libel against Israel. Arab and Islamic groups, as well as many leftist groups, are more than willing to jump into the fray. The preposterous and quite bizarre proposition presented today is that the State of Israel and its armed forces are deliberately and knowingly killing innocent Palestinian Arabs. Such lies serve the same purpose today as they did in the days of al-Husseini, not to mention in medieval times, namely as a means of fanning of the flames of hatred and stoking the fires of genocide against the Jews.

The anti-Jewish pogrom and riots of 1929 targeted the Jewish communities of Jerusalem, Motza, Hebron, Safad, Haifa, Tel Aviv, and Jaffa, as well as Jews living in the countryside. The British authorities responded to the Hebron slaughter in particular with a banishment of the entire Jewish community of Hebron. The British forcibly evacuated the Jews of Hebron to Jerusalem. The enactment of this decree by the British would leave Hebron ethnically cleansed of all of its indigenous Jews and would mark the first of many future ethnic cleansings in the region.

Abbady, a native Palestinian Jew and an acquaintance of al-Husseini at the time, documented the following comments attributed to al-Husseini:

> Remember, Abbady, this was and will remain an Arab land. We do not mind you natives of the country, but those alien invaders, the Zionists, will be massacred to the last man. We want no progress, no prosperity. Nothing but the sword will decide the fate of this country.

In December of 1931, al-Husseini, having further tightened his grip on Palestine and after having increased his influence in the Islamic world as a whole, organized and chaired what was called the All-Islamic Conference in Jerusalem, an event that would further enhance his image as a leader of all Arabs and Muslims. In attendance at the conference were pan-Arab leaders and representatives from various parts of the Arab and Muslim world including Tunisian Muslim leader Abd al-Aziz al-Tha'alibi, Indian Muslim leader Shawkat Ali, and Bosnian Muslim leaders Mehmed Spaho, the head of the Yugoslav Muslim Organization or JMO, Uzeiraga Hadzihasanovic, and Hadzi Mujaga Merhemic among others.

The All-Islamic Conference declared al-Husseini as president for life, which propelled him into further orbits of Arab and Islamic politics. The influence of al-Husseini would at this point reach to the far corners of the Arab world. In the coming years, he would use that influence in the service of the Nazi Third Reich. Leading up to that period, al-Husseini was assisting in the development and advancement of various political organizations in Arab capitals that were similar to his own al-Nadi al-Arabi, except with an increasingly Nazi coloration.

The period from the 1931 All-Islamic Conference to the 1937

al-Husseini-Eichmann meeting was a wild and rollicking time in Palestine. This was a period of unprecedented Jewish immigration coming in from Europe, which, due to the influence of Hitler, was growing increasingly ugly as a place for Jews to live. Nazism was on the ascent in Europe and was casting its totalitarian appeal across the Mediterranean and into Arab politics and into Arab minds and spirits.

The Zionists were doing all they could in those years to develop the Yishuv, or the Jewish community, as many of the institutions, including the Histadrut labor organization, the education system, and other institutions essential for a functioning sovereign state, were being established and solidified with a keen eye toward the day when Israel would achieve independence. While the Jewish settlers and the Zionist movement itself were mostly secular, a religious Jewish spirit nevertheless animated the ingathering of the exiles and a messianic fervor gripped the growing community. The dark clouds gathering over Europe added a sense of urgency to the atmosphere.

The Arab reaction to these developments was at first somewhat diffuse, even as al-Husseini continued to consolidate power over his rivals. Many and varied Arab political parties began to spring up and exert influence. Al-Husseini's own Palestine Arab Party stood for the expulsion of all Jewish settlers and an independent Arab Palestine as a step toward the pan-Arab *ummah*. The rival Nashashibi clan established the National Defense Party, which stood for an independent Palestine cooperating with the British. The Nashashibis rejected the pan-Arab *ummah*, sought an alliance with Emir Abdallah of Transjordan, and initially maintained a cooperative relationship with the Jewish Yishuv. The al-Istiqlal continued to regard Palestine as part of southern Syria. Other smaller and more regional parties also exerted influence.

The election of Hitler as chancellor of Germany on January 30, 1933, was an event that galvanized the entire Arab world, and this would serve to further accelerate al-Husseini's growing influence. Al-Husseini, the master organizer and single-minded charismatic leader, would accelerate his efforts to assist in the development of what would become distinctly Nazi-Arab-style organizations and political parties. In October of 1933, the same year Hitler came to power, al-Husseini played a role in the creation of Young Egypt, also known as the Green Shirts, which was headed by Ahmed Hussein and which included among its members a young Gamel Abdel Nasser, a protégé of al-Husseini and later president of Egypt. The Green Shirts adopted as their motto the Nazi-style slogan "One Folk, One Party, One Leader." Pro-Nazi parties also formed in Tunisia and Morocco in these prewar years.

Anton Saada, referred to as "the führer of the Syrian nation" by his followers, was head of the "Hisb-el-qaumi-el-suri," the Social Nationalist Party (PPS) of Syria established in Damascus. A Lebanese branch of the PPS would later give rise to various fascist-style Muslim militias and organizations, which would clash in the 1975 Lebanon Civil War as Lebanon disintegrated into warring Muslim and Christian Phalangist militias. The Phalangists were inspired by Italian fascism. A PPS branch, directed from Syria, had been previously implicated in the assassination of the Christian Lebanese President Pierre Gemayel in 1958. The PPS of Anton Saada proclaimed in its party platform "Syrians were the superior race by their very nature." Sami al-Joundi, a founder of the Syrian Ba'ath movement, wrote: "We were racists. We admired the Nazis. We were immersed in reading Nazi literature and books that were the

Mein Kampf by Adolf Hitler. Distributed by
Palestinian Authority—2003

source of the Nazi spirit. We were the first who thought of a translation of *Mein Kampf*. Anyone who lived in Damascus at that time was witness to the Arab inclination toward Nazism."

Nazism was wildly popular in the Arab world from day one. The first congratulatory telegrams to Hitler upon his election came from Arabs and were delivered to the German consulate in Jerusalem. These dispatches were quickly followed by telegrams of congratulation emanating from various Arab capitals. Al-Husseini conveyed to the German council in Jerusalem that "the Muslims inside and outside Palestine welcome the new regime of Germany and hope for the extension of the fascist, anti-democratic, governmental system to other countries." al-Husseini would proceed to establish a Palestinian Arab youth group at this time, which he called the Nazi Scouts.

The Nazis themselves were quite puzzled by this outpouring of support since, according to their unique and crackpot race mythology, the Arabs constituted an inferior race. A popular Arab song in the late 1930s included the melodic line, "No more Monsieur, no more Mister. In Heaven Allah, on Earth Hitler." Many Arab intellectuals and revisionists now explain this affinity the Arabs had for Hitler and Nazism with the assertion that this was because Nazi Germany was opposed to British and French colonialism in the Arab world.

There is not a shred of evidence to back this assertion up, as Hitler was on record as being pro-British and very much an Anglophile right up until and even beyond the September 1939 outbreak of the war between Britain and Germany. In *Mein Kampf*, Hitler wrote, "I as a man of Germanic blood, would, in spite of everything, rather see India under English rule than under any other. Just as lamentable are the hopes in any mythical uprising in Egypt . . . . As a volkish man, who appraises the value of men on a racial basis, I am prevented by mere knowledge of the racial inferiority of these so-called 'oppressed nations' from linking the destiny of my own people with theirs."

My contention is that the popularity of Nazism in the Arab world was traceable to various authoritarian aspects of the Arab and Islamic culture and faith. The Arab-Muslim concept of *ummah* or motherland has striking similarity to the Nazi concept of fatherland and *Lebensraum*. The Arab-Muslim concept of the caliph is similar to the Nazi concept of the führer. The Arab-Muslim concept of sharia is the equivalent of the Nazi concept of a centralized and hyper-nationalistic government controlling the rights of the people. Jihad is of a similar nature to blitz-krieg. Dar el-Islam is similar to the Thousand Year Reich.

Hitler's popularity in the Arab world was intense and immediate, and that popularity, as well as a cult personality following, endures to this day. The Arabs would go so far as to Islamicize Hitler's name, rendering it as Abu Ali, except in Egypt where Hitler would be known as Muhammad Haidar. Pro-Nazi Egyptians even claimed to have "found" the house where Hitler's mother was alleged to have been born in Tanta, Egypt. The site became a popular pilgrimage destination for Egyptians. The Young Egypt Green Shirts closely modeled themselves after the Nazi Party, using a variation of the sig heil salute, stormtroopers, torch-light processions, and terror campaigns against Egyptian political oppo-nents and Jews.

During the war, the Egyptian Green Shirts often acted as a fifth col-umn for the Nazis as many members of the secretive group conducted espionage and sabotage on behalf of the Third Reich and against the pro-British Egyptian government. Green Shirt activists sent intelligence information to the Nazi General Erwin Rommel, the famous Desert Fox, as his Afrika Korps fought in North Africa near the Egyptian border. When Rommel was able to reach the approaches of the Egyptian city of Alexandria, members of the Young Egypt Green Shirts used their coer-cive influence to paralyze the pro-British Cairo government to the point that Egypt was unable to lend much assistance to the beleaguered British during the battle of El Alamein. Anwar Sadat, the future Egyptian presi-dent and a young lieutenant and secret member of the Green Shirts dur-ing the war, was tried and imprisoned by the British as a Nazi spy.

Green Shirt member Gamel Abdel Nasser would later participate in the July 1952 officers' coup in Egypt. In the tradition of both Nazism and Communism, and following in al-Husseini's footsteps in Palestine, the Egyptian officers, upon seizing power, immediately banned all political opposition and stifled all dissent. Anwar Sadat, a protégé of Nasser, expressed admiration for Hitler in a letter to the Egyptian daily *Al Mussawar* on September 18, 1953, eight years after the defeat of the Third Reich.

Nazism remains a part of the fabric of life in Egypt today. The Egyptian president's ceremonial troops still wear helmets modeled after those worn by the Nazi Wehrmacht, and visiting heads of state are received at the Cairo airport by a goose-stepping military parade. Israeli

Prime Minister Menachem Begin, himself a survivor of the Nazi Holocaust, was greeted by Egyptian helmeted stormtroopers as he deplaned in Cairo to attend the funeral of Anwar Sadat in 1981. In 2001, an Egyptian columnist wrote in the government-sponsored *Al-Akhbar*: "Thank you, Hitler, of blessed memory, who on behalf of the Palestinians avenged in advance against the most vile criminals on Earth."

The Palestine Liberation Organization (PLO) maintained well-established and well-documented ties with postwar neo-Nazi organizations. Since the Oslo Accords and the establishment of the Palestinian Authority (PA) in the 1990s, the Palestinian political movement has made halfhearted attempts to camouflage some of the more blatant aspects of these associations, along with their strident admiration for Hitler and Nazism, so as to not offend the delicate sensibilities of their new American and Israeli leftist allies. This transparent marketing campaign did not, however, stop the August 1995 graduating class of PA police cadets, who would later participate in the mass murder of innocent Jews, to mark the occasion with a swearing in that included a straight-arm-style Nazi sig heil salute. Fawsi Salim el Mahdi, at the time a commander of "Tanzim 17," Arafat's elite praetorian guard that would later participate in suicide bombings against Jews, was known to his associates as "Abu Hitler" because he named his two sons Eichmann and Hitler.

Palestinian soldiers under Yasir Arafat doing Nazi salute—today.

The sinister and conspiratorial view of Zionism, the one that originated with Hitler and is described in *Mein Kampf*, prevails in much of the Arab world today. This view, heavily promoted by al-Husseini, resonates today among many left-wing circles as well. In *Mein Kampf*, this is what Hitler had to say about Zionism: "They [Zionists] do not have any intention to establish a Jewish state in Palestine in order to settle there. They only fight for one place in which they [can base] a central organization for carrying out their global plot, a city of refuge for criminals and a training center for the scoundrels of the future." I emphatically reiterate that the Zionist movement was, is, and shall for evermore remain nothing more and nothing less than the national movement of the Jewish people to achieve a sovereign homeland in Palestine.

Celebrating the signing of the Camp David Accords, 1978, in the White House Rose Garden: Israeli Prime Minister Menachem Begin (right, back to camera), American President Jimmy Carter (center), Egyptian President Anwar Sadat (left)

The Muslim Brotherhood

Hassan al-Banna, founder of the Muslim Brotherhood

In 1928, Hassan al-Banna, an Egyptian schoolteacher, established a secret society that he called the Muslim Brotherhood, al-Ikhwan al-Muslimeen, in Cairo. In 1935, Abdul Rahman al-Banna, a key member of the society and the brother of the founder traveled to Palestine to establish direct contact with al-Husseini. The Brotherhood would proceed to work in tandem with al-Husseini as irregulars, and volunteers recruited from the ranks of the Brotherhood would be organized and sent into Palestine with the goal of helping al-Husseini launch the 1936-1939 riots, known as the Arab Revolt. During World War II, the Brotherhood, with branches in several Arab capitals at that point, maintained an informal espionage relationship with the Third Reich. In 1945, Muslim Brotherhood member Sa'id Ramadan established the first formal branch of the Brotherhood in Jerusalem. In the 1948 Israel War of Independence, the Brotherhood once again flooded the region with irregulars and volunteers.

The Muslim Brotherhood is a pan-Arab secret society that believes in the ultimate virtue of a one world utopia, or Dar el-Islam, under the forceful guidance of the Islamic scimitar. As was the case with al-Husseini, the Third Reich also influenced and supported the

Brotherhood in the 1930s and 1940s. Today the Brotherhood is backed by Saudi Arabian petro-dollars and is behind many secretive terrorist groups, including Hamas and Islamic Jihad. Muhammad Sa'id al-Ashmawy, the former chief justice of Egypt's High Criminal Court, best described the Muslim Brotherhood when he referred to its ideology as a "perversion of Islam" and spoke of "the fascistic ideology" that infuses the world view of the Brotherhood, "their total (if not totalitarian) way of life . . . [and] their fantastical reading of the Koran."

Around the same time that the Muslim Brotherhood was established in Egypt, a similar secretive group of brethren formed in Saudi Arabia. The Saudi group based its faith on a puritanical interpretation of Koranic passages and follows a particular discipline known as Wahabism. Both the Egyptian-based Muslim Brotherhood and the Saudi Arabian Wahabi radicals borrowed heavily from an Islamic movement called the Salafiyya, which believes that true Muslims must tow a path in strict accordance with that of the seventh-century Islam of the Prophet Mohammed.

Both groups were reacting at the time to the introduction of modernity and democracy in the Islamic world as ideas were circulating that emanated from outside. Both the Brotherhood and the Wahabis came to believe that these Western ideas posed a threat to Islam. Not only would these groups conspire to punish the "infidels" that they felt were threatening the *ummah*, but they would also threaten Muslim leaders and intellectuals who dared to embrace or even conduct relations of any kind with this ominous outside world from their perspective. These groups insisted on the strict maintenance of what they perceived to be a pure form of Islamic practice and way of life. Their obsession with a perfect purity of thought and action found resonance in the quite similar approach that the Nazis took toward the concept of racial purity.

One core belief of the Muslim Brotherhood is that in order to be ultimately successful, Islam must achieve a total victory over Judaism in order to make way for the emergence of a unified pan-Arab utopia. It should be reiterated at this point that Islam could be and is employed by the extremists as a political and military apparatus as much a spiritual one. This idea goes back to the seventh century, when Muslim Arabs had stormed out of the Arabian Desert. The desert faith was subsequently spread not through means of peaceable conversion, which was the way Christianity was mostly spread in the Roman Empire and in Europe, but through bloody coercion and conquest.

Toward the end of the seventh century, Arab armies forcibly conquered the well-established and urbane Christian societies of Palestine, Syria, Egypt, North Africa, Spain, and later Asia Minor and the Balkans. Tens of millions of indigenous Christians in these conquered lands were given the option of conversion, servitude, or slaughter, and tens of millions of Christians were either forcibly converted or slaughtered in a slow motion holocaust that was carried out over a millennia and that continues to this day. Entire Christian civilizations were virtually wiped out. As a young Ottoman officer, al-Husseini most likely observed first-hand the genocide against the Armenian and Greek Christians of Asia Minor.

The Muslim Brotherhood specifically believes that Islam is engaged in an eternal conflict with the Jews and that ultimate victory is essential in order to preserve the *ummah* or motherland. This mystical view of Jews dovetailed with that of the virtually identical Nazi view. The Muslim Brotherhood traced the conflict between Islam and Judaism back to the days of the Prophet Mohammed, when the substantial Jewish community of the city of Yathrib, later renamed Medina after the Muslim conquest, rejected Mohammed's ministry and chose instead to remain loyal to Judaism. In *Arabs and History* historian Bernard Lewis offers some background into the early stages of the conflict:

> Jewish tribes from the north, especially the Banu Nadir and Banu Quraiza, some 280 miles north of Mecca, had originally settled the city of Medina. The comparative richness of the town attracted an infiltration of pagan Arabs who came at first as clients of the Jews and ultimately succeeded in dominating them. The town was torn by the feuds of the rival Arab tribes of Aus and Khazraj, with the Jews maintaining an uneasy balance of power. The latter, engaged mainly in agriculture and handicrafts, were economically and culturally superior to the Arabs, and were consequently disliked . . . as soon as the Arabs had attained unity through the agency of Muhammad they attacked and ultimately eliminated the Jews.

In *The Tradition of Islam*, Alfred Guillaume, the nineteenth century British Arabist and the author of the universally respected English translation of seventh-century Muslim writer Ibn Ishaq's *Sirat Rasul Allah*, known in English as *The Life of Muhammad*, explains:

At the dawn of Islam the Jews dominated the economic life of the Hijaz [Arabia]. They held all the best land . . . at Medina they must have formed at least half of the population. There was also a Jewish settlement to the north of the Gulf of Aqaba. . . . Jewish prosperity was a challenge to the Arabs, particularly the Quraysh at Mecca and . . . at Medina.

In the process of militarily subduing Arabia, the Prophet and his followers increased their wealth by confiscating the land and property of Jewish merchants. The word "booty" derives from an Arabic word that means confiscated property. The gathering of booty was explicitly allowed and even condoned, as is indicated by passages in the Koran. The pillaging of the lands and property of the Arabian Jewish tribes, along with their expulsions, forced conversions, murders, and wholesale slaughters, would later become standard practice for advancing Islamic forces as they overran Christian, Hindu, Buddhist, and other populations viewed as standing in the path of the achievement of Dar el-Islam. Regarding the slaughter of the Jews of Khaibar, an Arabic Jewish settlement made up of Jews who had already fled from advancing Arabic forces, Alfred Guillaume, in his translation of Ibn Ishaq's *Sirat Rasul Allah*, wrote:

> They had irritated him [Muhammad] by their refusal to recognize him as a prophet. . . .The existence of pockets of disaffected Jews in and around his base was a cause of uneasiness and they had to be eliminated if he [Muhammad] was to wage war without anxiety . . . A tribe of Jews in the neighborhood of Medina fell under suspicion of treachery and was forced to lay down their arms and evacuate their settlements. Valuable land and much booty fell into the hands of the Muslims. The neighboring tribe of Qurayza, who were soon to suffer annihilation, made no move to help their co-religionists, and their allies, the Aus, were afraid to give them active support.

The Prophet Mohammed made plain his view of the Jews when he declared at the time, according to the authoritative Islamic text "Muwatta, in al-Zurkani" (commentary IV p. 71), "Two religions may not dwell together on the Arabian Peninsula." Abu Bakr and Omar, two caliphs who were immediate successors of the Prophet Mohammed, both proceeded to forcibly convert, evacuate, or exterminate the entire Jewish population of northern Arabia. On this issue, the Koran says the following:

> . . . Some you slew and others you took captive. He [Allah] made you masters of their [the Jews'] land, their houses and their goods, and of yet another land [Khaibar] on which you had never set foot before. Truly, Allah has power over all things.

From a fundamentalist Muslim perspective, the refusal of the Jews of Yathrib to convert to Islam during the life of the Prophet Mohammed was viewed as a challenge to the legitimacy of the Prophet himself and as an impediment and threat to the advancement of the message of the Prophet. It should be admitted that some of these same ideas have crept into Christianity at various times in history. Some Christians have believed that by refusing to accept the ministry of Jesus, the Jews presented a challenge to the legitimacy of His Messiahship. The difference between the Muslim and Christian view on this issue is that nowhere in the New Testament are Christians ordered by Jesus or any of His disciples to forcibly convert or kill Jews, nor are Christians encouraged to confiscate their property. While there is much sin in Christian history, nevertheless, Christianity clearly does not order that the Jew, or anyone else who refuses to submit or be converted, be in any way coerced, let alone slaughtered.

The early Muslim, as reflected in the beliefs of the Muslim Brotherhood today, believed that the Jew, by virtue of his refusal to accept the teachings of the Prophet Mohammed, was conspiring to abolish Islam and prevent its success. While the submitting Jew living in the Islamic *ummah* and submitting to a degree of sharia was allowed to live as a *dhimmi* or second-class citizen, and required to pay a special annual *jizya* tax, which bestowed upon him the privilege of living for another year as a Jew, the sovereign Jew, living in a Jewish state, free of sharia, exercising political, religious and cultural rights, and enjoying all the benefits of sovereignty, as is the case in Israel today, is entirely another matter altogether from the perspective of the Brotherhood.

The Muslim Brotherhood views its ongoing conflict with Israel as a spiritual conflict between Islam and Judaism, as opposed to a strictly military conflict. The fact that Israel is also a secularized Western society adds salt to the wound for the fundamentalist Islamic Muslim Brotherhood, which feels threatened by any and all influences they perceive as emanating from outside the Muslim world. This sense of threat also applies to surrounding non-Muslim states as well as to the more secular Western Arab and Muslim governments. Like al-Husseini in Palestine, the Muslim Brotherhood has engaged in violent conflicts and assassinations against secular Muslim leaders, as was the case with the Muslim Brotherhood assassination of Egyptian President Anwar Sadat in 1981.

The emblem of the Brotherhood is a Koran crossed by a sword and its influence extends to the far corners of the Muslim world today. Islamic Jihad, a secretive branch of the Brotherhood, maintains direct links to bin Laden's Al Qaeda network. Hamas is a direct offshoot of the Muslim Brotherhood, as is the banking firm Al Taqwa, implicated by the U.S. in funneling support to Osama bin Laden and the September 11, 2001 terrorists. Youssef Nada, chairman of Al Taqwa, joined the Muslim Brotherhood during World War II when he was recruited, along with other Muslim Brothers, by Nazi military intelligence for espionage against the British colonial government in Egypt.

The Brotherhood remains the font of terror in the region.

The secretive Brotherhood continues to be the primary repository of the most extreme practitioners of a virulent strain of Islam, one that seeks to impose itself on others through the most violent means. There is a long and interesting intermingling between the faith and ideology of the Brotherhood and that of the Nazis and later the Communists. One visible result of this intermingling is a merge between the traditional victimization mythologies, which hold that religious Muslims are somehow under siege by the outside world, with the Nazi victimology mythology, which held that Germans were somehow victimized by the existence of the Jews. The Communist variant of this victimization scenario holds that citizens are somehow exploited by the existence of the wealthy.

The Grossmufti vom Jerusalem

The first known direct and significant contact between an important Nazi official and an important Arab official in the Middle East occurred in 1936 when al-Husseini met with Francois Genoud, later known as the Swiss banker of the Third Reich, in Palestine. A long-term professional and personal relationship between al-Husseini and Genoud would ensue. According to the British author and researcher Gitta Sereny, al-Husseini "would consider Genoud a confidant until his death in 1974." *Le Monde* correspondent Jean-Claude Buhrer wrote that Genoud "traveled to Berlin frequently during the war to see his friend the Grand Mufti, and visited him afterward many times in Beirut." Sereny wrote that al-Husseini "entrusted Genoud with the management of his enormous financial affairs."

Francois Genoud, from Lausanne, Switzerland, had met Hitler before he became chancellor in 1932. In 1934, Genoud joined the pro-Nazi Swiss National Front. During the war, Genoud lent financial assistance to al-Husseini and his Berlin-based Nazi-Muslim government-in-exile by financially supporting the anti-Jewish propaganda campaign al-Husseini spearheaded in the Arab world from his Berlin headquarters. Genoud was made an honorary member of the Nazi Waffen-SS and was awarded a

Gold Badge by Hitler, honors that he held proudly for the rest of his politically active life. On May 30, 1996, the eighty-one-year-old Genoud committed suicide as Jewish leaders and Swiss banking officials were zeroing in on his decades of laundering money through Swiss bank accounts that had been looted by the Nazis from European Jews. Genoud remained a fully witting, steadfast, and unrepentant Nazi to the very end.

In 1935, one year before making contact with the Swiss-Nazi financier, al-Husseini received millions of dollars from the Italian Fascist Foreign Minister Count Galeazzo Ciano for the purpose of poisoning the water wells of Tel Aviv. Years later, Ciano told the German ambassador to Italy that "for years he maintained constant relations with the Grand Mufti of which his secret fund could tell a tale. The practical return on this gift of millions had not been exactly great and had really been confined to the occasional destruction of pipelines, which in most cases could be quickly repaired."

In 1936-1939, with the help of the Muslim Brotherhood and with Nazi financing, al-Husseini played a key role in the riots against both the British and the Jews of Palestine, riots known in Israel as the Arab Revolt. Al-Husseini, perhaps benefiting from an infusion of cash after meeting with the Nazi banker that same year, was appointed as head of the radical Arab Higher Committee, which directly planned and organized the riots. On July 15, 1937, six days before the outbreak of the rioting, al-Husseini visited the Nazi Ambassador Doehle, the German consul in Jerusalem. Herr Doehle reported on his meeting with al-Husseini to his superiors in Berlin, stating, "The Grand Mufti stressed Arab sympathy for the new Germany and expressed the hope that Germany was sympathetic toward the Arab fight against Jewry and was prepared to support it."

The Arab Revolt was launched in Jaffa on April 19, 1936, as a result of a false rumor, spread by al-Husseini's secret network, that four Arabs, three men and one woman, had been slaughtered by Jews in Tel Aviv. The rumormongers placed the four corpses at the local British-run hospital. Like clockwork, an orchestrated mob of thousands descended on the British Mandate offices. In spite of the fact that the British escorted an Arab delegation to the hospital in an attempt to prove the falseness of this blood libel, the rioting nevertheless quickly grew in intensity with crowds shrieking *"Itbach el-Yahud,"* "kill the Jews." The carnage quickly spread to other Jewish communities and the Arab riots of 1936–1939 were thus launched.

In the course of this long and bloody revolt, the region's first suicide bombers were introduced, and targeted for death were Arab
opponents of al-Husseini and his allies. Al-Husseini had at this point
clearly demonstrated a full and enthusiastic embrace of Nazism and
the Nazi idea of a "systematic extermination" of Jews, as well as a sup-
pression of Arabs he suspected of disloyalty to him and his increasingly Nazi agenda. During this period, the remnant of active Arab
moderates in Palestine were either murdered, driven out of public life,
or driven into exile, never again to return to Palestine. The same phe-
nomena occurred in other Arab states during this period, as increasingly radicalized Arab elites moved closer to Hitler.

In the midst of the Arab Revolt in Palestine, in November 1936, the
British sent Lord Peel as the head of a commission for the purpose of
interviewing various parties to the conflict. Peel intended to file a report
to the British government that would serve as a blueprint for British gov-
ernance of Palestine as well as a long-term plan for Palestinian independence. The Peel Commission interview with al-Husseini left little doubt
regarding his agenda. Al-Husseini made clear to the commission that he
expected the establishment of an all-Arab-Muslim state in Palestine and
that as head of this state he would summarily evict the approximately four
hundred thousand Jewish settlers. A remnant of indigenous Jews would
be permitted to remain, al-Husseini made clear, and would be expected
to return to a traditional *dhimmi* status (*Appendix D*).

Arab leaders at the time and Arab revisionists ever since point an
accusatory finger at the Zionists, with the ridiculous claim that they had
conspired to evict all Arabs from Palestine at this time. In fact, it was
al-Husseini who made clear his intention to do just that regarding the
Jews in his 1936 interview with the Peel Commission. The commission
report, prompted by the intransigent attitude on the part of al-Husseini,
as well as the increasing radicalization of the Palestinian Arabs, recommended as a solution to the growing conflict another partitioning of
Palestine west of the Jordan into an Arab and a Jewish sector. The first
partition, to reiterate, occurred in 1921 when the British Mandate of
Palestine was divided along the Jordan River between the Jews and the
Arabs. The Peel Commission report recommended that al-Husseini's
chief rival, the Hashemite Emir Abdallah, the regent of Transjordan, or
Palestine east of the Jordan, play a prominent role in the future of the
Arab sector of the new partition.

The uncompromising al-Husseini responded to the idea of partition by totally rejecting any recognition of any rights for the Jews whatsoever. To further drive home that rejection, al-Husseini proceeded to use his position to further ratchet up the revolt. This rejection of the Peel Committee recommendations as motivated by the absolute and imperialist position on the part of al-Husseini that the Jews deserved absolutely no sovereign rights whatsoever in Palestine. This rejection would mark the first of many lost opportunities for the Palestinian Arabs to obtain sovereignty west of the Jordan River.

As part of a ratcheting up of violence stemming from the rejection of the Peel Commission recommendations, Palestinian Arab leaders and clerics who had opposed al-Husseini would now come under increased assault. Arabs assassinated by al-Husseini-inspired death squads during the riots of 1936-1939 would include Palestinian Arab leaders Sheikh Daoud Ansari, imam of the Al Aqsa Mosque; Sheikh Ali Nur el-Khatib; Sheikh Nusbi Abdal Rahim, Council of Muslim Religious Court; Sheikh Abdul el-Badoui from Acre; Sheikh el-Namouri from Hebron; Nasr el-Din Nassr, mayor of Hebron; and eleven *mukhtars*, or community leaders, who were murdered along with their entire families by al-Husseini's roving killers.

Many fair-minded and reasonable Palestinian Arabs did support the Peel Commission recommendation of partition, a recommendation that eventually bore fruit in 1948. Whether these moderates actually believed that such a partition was actually proper and reasonable or if they were at this point motivated by a more tactical and situational approach is open to question. Al-Husseini, while publicly posing as a moderate for British consumption and in order to preserve his office while still in British Palestine, continued nevertheless to agitate for violence behind the scenes and continued to use his stature in the Arab world to agitate against the partition plan as recommended by the commission.

In 1937, in the volatile months following the Peel Commission controversy, Nazi SA Obergruppenführer Reinhard Heydrich sent the infamous Nazi SS Hauptscharführer Adolf Eichmann and his assistant Nazi SS Oberscharführer Herbert Hagen to Palestine as special envoys on a mission where they would meet with al-Husseini. The two Nazis would arrive on October 2, 1937, on the liner *Romania* disembarking in Haifa. Discussions between Eichmann and al-Husseini during this visit, which lasted less than forty-eight hours due to British restrictions, most likely included the so-called "Jewish question," given the fact that both al-Husseini and Eichmann shared an obsession with the Jews. This meeting, the first of many meetings between Eichmann and al-Husseini in a relationship that would stretch into the war years, marked another critical turning point in terms of Nazi influence in the Arab world.

Eichmann also met at the time with a Zionist Hagana agent, Feivel Polkes, who desperately lobbied him for an increase in the number of German Jews that would be allowed to emigrate from Nazi Germany into Palestine. In his meeting with Eichmann, Polkes argued that the immigration of German Jews into Palestine would provide a means by which Nazi Germany could solve its so-called "Jewish question." There apparently were many Nazi officials in the years leading up to the outbreak of the war, including even possibly Hitler himself, who were at one point or another open to the idea of allowing Jewish immigration into Palestine or elsewhere as a means of ridding Europe of Jews.

Upon his return to Germany, after a brief stopover in Cairo, Eichmann filed a report to his superiors recommending that the question of allowing Jewish emigration out of Europe into Palestine or anywhere else not be considered as an option. Eichmann wrote glowingly of "the national and racial conscience" that he observed while among the Arabs. He reported that "Nazi flags fly in Palestine and they adorn their houses with Swastikas and portraits of Hitler." Clearly Eichmann, and the Nazi command, had decided at this point to cultivate further ties with the most extreme elements in the Arab countries.

Adolf Eichmann was apparently quite learned in the Jewish religion and in Jewish affairs, as he reportedly had been obsessed with all things Jewish since his childhood and had achieved a good command of the Hebrew language. As head of the Department of Jewish Affairs in the Gestapo, 1941-1945, Eichmann would be one of the key players in the Holocaust against the Jews. As the chief of operations, this close associate of al-Husseini's would go on to oversee the transport of up to three million Jews to concentration camps in Nazi Germany and in Nazi-occupied Europe. Eichmann was by all accounts one of the main masterminds of the program to liquidate the Jews of Europe.

Also in 1937, September 8-9, al-Husseini organized an all-Arab conference in Baludan, Syria, attended by four hundred delegates from across the Islamic world as well as one hundred and twenty-four

Palestinian Arabs. On September 26, Lewis Andrews, the British district commissioner of the Galilee, was murdered in Nazareth by members of a radical and secretive terrorist organization called Ikhwan al-Qassam. This group was named after the anti-British Sheikh Izz al-Din al-Qassam, who, as head of a group called the Black Hand, had been killed by the British in 1935. The British responded to this provocation by arresting several Arabs and exiling them to the Seychelles Islands, disbanding the Arab Higher Committee, and stripping al-Husseini of all of his positions except that of grand mufti of Jerusalem. On October 13, al-Husseini slipped out of his headquarters in the Temple Mount and fled to Lebanon.

In French Lebanon, out of reach of the British and with nothing to lose in Palestine, al-Husseini set up shop in the town of Dhauq Mika'il, where he continued to control what was left of the Arab Higher Committee, now in exile, as well as all Arab officeholders in Palestine. Al-Husseini achieved a controlling position as well in the Damascus-based Central Committee of the Jihad and began to directly arrange for murder and sabotage operations in Palestine. No longer restrained by a need to preserve his governing authority in the British Mandate, al-Husseini, by use of his secret network in Palestine, now acted with impunity against his enemies, both political and personal, both Arab and Jew. As a result, al-Husseini, now fully backed by Nazi money, entered into a more murderous and violent stage in his career.

Murder and sabotage operations would increase and reach a crescendo in Palestine in 1938, as would the carrying out of direct orders from al-Husseini to murder moderate Arab leaders and those with whom al-Husseini sought to settle scores. During this period, a group of Arab intellectuals from Haifa sent a representative to meet with al-Husseini in Lebanon and to appeal to him to stop ordering the murders of Arabs, an appeal that was rejected by al-Husseini. By the summer of 1939, exhausted Arabs cooperating with and armed by the British formed "peace bands" in order to put down the revolt.

The answer to the "Jewish question" in Europe was becoming clearer in 1939. The British, in another attempt at appeasement of the more extreme pro-Nazi element in the Middle East, issued the White Paper for Palestine. Jewish immigration would now be severely restricted on the eve of the outbreak of World War II. The White Paper, in violation of international law, represented a complete repudiation and reversal of the Balfour Declaration, the Faisal-Weizmann Agreement, and the raison d'être of the League of Nations British Mandate for Palestine. The White Paper essentially rendered the Mandate technically null and void. The White Paper, which formally abolished the Jewish national home, marked what should have been a major victory for al-Husseini and his agenda, yet the White Paper didn't go far enough for al-Husseini, who wanted all immigration of Jews to be completely stopped, followed by the establishment of an all-Arab sovereign Palestine that would be stripped of all Jews except a small number of *dhimmis*. Al-Husseini rejected the White Paper.

Once again, the extremism and zeal of this one man, over the objections of many of his colleagues on the Arab Higher Committee meeting in Lebanon, resulted in the loss of what British Colonial Secretary Malcolm McDonald called "a golden opportunity" for the Arab extremists to abolish Jewish Palestine. As would become par for the course in these matters, and in a pattern that is followed by Palestinian Arab leadership to this day, al-Husseini decided to reverse himself and had the audacity to accept the White Paper six years later, in 1945, after the conclusion of the Second World War and the failure of Hitler's promise to al-Husseini that he would assist in liquidating Palestinian Jewry. After the Holocaust against the Jews of Europe, and given al-Husseini's own degree of collaboration in that evil effort, it was rather late in the day, to put it mildly, for al-Husseini to be suddenly coming out in favor of the White Paper, especially in light of al-Husseini's own direct participation in the Nazi Holocaust.

In 1939, the British had decided to sell out the Jews in response to both the growing power of fascism in Europe on the eve of hostilities and in response to the popularity of Nazism in the Arab world. They thought they could buy support from the most extreme element in Arab society. The White Paper was yet another milestone in a policy of appeasement by Western powers to Islamic extremism. The British had already unsuccessfully tried to appease Hitler in Europe when the liberal British Prime Minister Neville Chamberlain signed the 1938 Munich Accords, which allowed the Nazis to wolf down a large slice of Czechoslovakia.

Most of Europe's Jews would now be effectively and almost completely sealed into Nazi-occupied Europe, with few opportunities for escape. The Holocaust would then ensue, with the Western democracies shouldering a great deal of responsibility for having colluded with the Nazis in slamming the European door shut. By formally rejecting the British White Paper, al-Husseini had furthered a pattern of intransigence and fanaticism that has plagued relations ever since between Israel and the Arabs. The British White Paper amounted to a promise by the British that an all-Arab Palestine would come into existence in ten years. Al-Husseini responded to the British appeasement by moving closer to the Nazis and in the process he squandered an opportunity to achieve his diabolical goal for Palestine.

In 1938, as a follow up to the al-Husseini-Eichmann meeting, Nazi Admiral Wilhelm Canaris, the head of the German Abwehr Intelligence Division, had put the exiled al-Husseini on his payroll. Al-Husseini would now serve as an agent for Nazi political, financial, and military interests in the Middle East. Also shortly after the meeting, the Arab uprising against the British, the Jews, and unsympathetic Palestinian Arabs would be ratcheted up in Palestine, an uprising that would continue intermittently until hostilities broke out between Nazi Germany and Britain in 1939 and which would further consolidate the power of al-Husseini and his followers in Palestine. During this period, the members of the moderate Palestinian Arab National Defense Party, made up primarily of members of the moderate Nashashibi clan, a rival of the al-Husseini clan, either dropped out of public life or went into exile. The Arab revolt would result in the deaths of 2,652 Jews, 618 British, and 6,953 Arabs.

After the Eichmann meeting, and his deportation from Palestine, al-Husseini sent his personal agent, Dr. Said Imam, who was fluent in German and who had been in regular contact with the German consulate in Beirut, directly to Berlin. In a letter carried by Imam, al-Husseini wrote that if Germany would "support the Arab independence movement ideologically and materially," then al-Husseini would arrange for "disseminating National Socialist ideas in the Arab-Islamic world, combating Communism, which appears to be spreading gradually, by employing all possible means." al-Husseini promised the Germans "continuing acts of terrorism in all French colonial and mandated territories inhabited by Arabs or Mohammedans." In the event of a Nazi victory, he swore "to utilize only German capital and intellectual resources." al-Husseini dutifully embraced crackpot Nazi racial mythology when he wrote of the importance of maintaining a separation of Semitic and Aryan races. In the letter al-Husseini referred to the importance of "maintaining and respecting the national convictions of both peoples."

Al-Husseini fled from Lebanon to Iraq on October 13, 1939, after the French government in Syria had placed him under surveillance. This occurred one month after the September 1939 outbreak of the war. With the war now underway, Nazi intrigue in the Arab world, with al-Husseini playing the pivotal role, would now go into high gear, and one of the results would be the 1941 Nazi-backed coup against the pro-British government in Iraq led by General Rashid Ali al-Gailani.

Amin al-Husseini with Rashid Ali al-Gailani, leader of the 1941 pro-Nazi Iraqi coup

Al-Husseini was welcomed into Baghdad at the time with cheering crowds and was hailed as a pan-Arab hero and a defender of the faith with the same zeal that Hitler was being hailed at Nazi rallies. Upon his arrival, he immediately launched into political intrigue by organizing and effectively gaining control of the secretive, pan-Arab and pro-Nazi Iraqi Arab National Party. The agenda of this party was to link up with likeminded groups in Syria, Transjordan, and cis-Jordan (Palestine) and, with Nazi backing, throw out the colonial powers and form an independent and united Arab *ummah*.

Al-Husseini also set up at this time the Iraqi Committee of Seven, which included Iraqi General Rashid Ali al-Gailani, and three of the four generals that made up what came to be known as the Golden Square. The committee met at al-Husseini's house in the spring of 1941 to plan the pro-Nazi coup against the pro-British government. In the months leading up to the coup, al-Husseini arranged for representatives of the coup plotters to meet with Franz von Papen, the Nazi ambassador to Turkey, and Joachim von Ribbentrop, the Nazi foreign minister.

Nineteen forty-one was a climactic and pivotal year in the war between the Allied forces and Nazi Germany. The Battle of Britain was raging and Nazi Field Marshall Erwin Rommel, known as the Desert Fox, was advancing on Egypt. In June of 1941, the Nazis would launch Operation Barbarossa, which involved a full frontal assault on their erstwhile ally the Soviet Union. The Nazi blitzkrieg would soon be advancing toward the Russian Caucasus. Early in 1941, al-Husseini's German-speaking personal envoy, Uthman Kamal Haddad, embarked from Iraq on a secret mission to Berlin, traveling under the pseudonym Max Muller with a letter that he personally delivered to Hitler on January 20, 1941. In the letter, al-Husseini requested that Hitler issue a public declaration of support for Arab independence. Al-Husseini presented himself in the letter as the only Arab leader in a position to speak to the Nazis on behalf of all Arabs. Regarding Palestine, al-Husseini wrote:

> His Excellence is well aware of the problem faced by this country, which has also suffered from the deceitful actions of the English. They attempted to place an additional obstacle before the unity and independence of the Arab states by abandoning it to world Jewry, this dangerous enemy whose secret weapon . . . finance, corruption and intrigue . . . were aligned with British daggers . . . Full of unvanquished faith, the Arabs of Palestine fought with the most elementary mutual hatred of the English and the Jews . . . From an international point of view, the Jews owe allegiance to England, in the hope that, after her victory, she will be able to realize their dreams in Palestine and in the neighboring Arab countries.

On April 1, 1941, the well-planned pro-Nazi coup d'etat was launched and it brought General Rashid Ali al-Gailini to power in Iraq. On May 9, 1941, al-Husseini issued a fatwa of jihad against the British, declaring Great Britain to be "the greatest foe of Islam." The British responded to the coup by releasing Jewish Irgun members, including David Raziel, from prison. Along with a group of his fellow Irgun fighters, Raziel went to Baghdad for the purpose of committing sabotage on behalf of the British and killing al-Husseini. In May of 1941, German and Italian fighter-bombers landed in Vichy French-controlled Syria, where they obtained permission from Rashid Ali to fly to Iraq to help the coup and on May 20, Raziel was killed when his car was bombed by one of these German fighter-bombers. The fighter-bombers had arrived too late to seriously alter events. The pro-Nazi coup collapsed at the end of May in the face of a gathering British-Arab advance.

Al-Husseini blamed the defeat of the pro-Nazi coup on the ancient and indigenous Jewish community of Iraq, a community that could trace its lineage as far back as the period of captivity of ancient Judah by the Babylonian King Nebuchadnezzar, as described in the Bible. The pro-British Hashemite regent of Iraq, Abd al-Illah, returned to Baghdad on June 1, 1941, and the crowd that gathered to welcome him and to celebrate the end of the pro-Nazi regime quickly turned into a murderous pogrom against the Iraqi Jews largely thanks to the slander spread by al-Husseini. Approximately six hundred Jews were murdered in areas ranging across the length and breadth of Iraq, and Jewish shops and homes were looted in the first substantial anti-Jewish action in Iraq in centuries. This pogrom is known to Sephardic Jews as the Fahud and is comparable in its ferocity to the Nazi Kristallnacht in Germany. A committee of inquiry would later implicate al-Husseini as an instigator of the riot. In an article entitled "The Fifth Column," al-Husseini wrote of the Jews of Iraq:

> The Fifth Column had a great influence on the failure of the Iraqi movement, and was comprised of many elements, most importantly, the Jews of Iraq. During the fighting, George Antonius [Christian Arab nationalist and author] told me that the Jews employed in the telephone department were recording important and official telephone conversations and passing them on to the British embassy in Baghdad. Jewish workers in the post and telegram departments acted in a similar fashion, forwarding the messages and letters that they received to the embassy.

This was not the first time al-Husseini had indulged in propagating a sinister Jewish conspiracy theory as a means of fomenting anti-Jewish violence, nor would it be the last. Similar charges against "the Jews" had already been used by al-Husseini to effectively fuel pogroms and riots in Palestine. The bloody slaughters of Iraqi Jews also proved to be profitable to al-Husseini in terms of raising large sums of money from like-minded anti-Jewish sources. Scapegoating the Jews also served as a means to explain and justify the continuing slide toward totalitarianism that was occurring in the Arab world generally. Jews could be blamed for virtually anything negative that was occurring as the increasingly fascist governments tightened their iron grip. In his memoirs, al-Husseini would also blame the defeat of Germany in World War I on the Jews and used this conspiracy theory to support and justify his participation in the Holocaust. He wrote as follows:

> In return for a declaration [the Balfour Declaration], the Jews took it upon themselves to serve Britain and its policies, and to do their utmost to secure a British victory in the war. In pursuit of this aim, Jews played a central role in the acts of sabotage and destructive propaganda inside Germany at the end of the [First World War] . . .This is the principle reason for Hitler's war against the Jews, and his hatred toward them. They brought disaster on Germany, and caused its defeat in the war—despite the fact that it had the advantage from a military point of view.

The murderous Iraqi riot would mark the beginning of the end for a Jewish community that pre-dated the Arab invasion and occupation of Iraq by up to a half a millennia. Amin al-Husseini, while residing in Baghdad, had petitioned Hitler to "recognize the right of the Arabs to solve the Jewish Question . . . in the same manner as in the Axis countries."

The influence that al-Husseini and his Nazi-inspired coup had on Iraq should not be discounted. Founded by the progressive King Faisal ibn Hussein, Iraq was, up until that point, moving toward becoming a sovereign and modern state. The regressive ideas of al-Husseini were instrumental in terms of introducing a radical form of pan-Arabism and Nazism into Iraq. The philosophy furthered by al-Husseini included the concept of an absolute authoritarian ruler. This concept was based on the Nazi idea of *Führerprinzip*, a principle that would later be exercised in Iraq by Saddam Hussein to the maximum degree.

Salah al-Din al-Sabbagh, one of the pro-Nazi Iraqi coup plotters, acknowledged the pan-Arab principle when he stated, "I do not believe in the democracy of the English nor in the Nazism of the Germans nor in the Bolshevism of the Russians. I am an Arab Muslim." The pan-Arab concept of a greater Arab *ummah* resonated with the Nazi concept of the Thousand Year Reich, which was the essential reason why, along with strategic considerations, the pan-Arabists and the Nazis found themselves in a natural alliance. The influence of al-Husseini and his Nazi backers has reverberated in Iraq ever since.

By 1941, with the war raging in Europe, the Nazis had become fully cognizant of the strategic importance of a Nazi-Arab alliance and there is substantial evidence to indicate that they considered al-Husseini to be their most trusted friend and conduit in the Arab world. The Nazi view of the Arabs would suddenly undergo an upgrade at this point. This is reflected in a change in the racial status of Arabs in crackpot Nazi racial mythology. Arabs would suddenly go from being viewed by the Nazis as a primitive people, as Hitler was known to have described the Arabs as "lacquered half-apes who ought to be whipped," to a lower race, but nevertheless a cut above Jews, Gypsies, and blacks, and with Nordic influences. Hitler was on record as stating that he believed that the fair-haired, blue-eyed al-Husseini probably had "more than one Aryan among his ancestors and one who may be descended from the best Roman stock."

One of the pro-Nazi Iraqi coup plotters in 1941 and a confidant of al-Husseini's was Saddam Hussein's uncle General Khairallah Tulfah, who would later become Saddam's guardian, mentor, and father-in-law. Clearly Saddam Hussein was tutored in the al-Husseini brand of Muslim-Nazism by his uncle from an early age, and would become one of the most devout and effective practitioners of al-Husseini-inspired Nazi-pan-Arabism, as his career would attest.

Al-Husseini proceeded to flee from the advancing British-Arab forces, along with the Iraqi pro-Nazi dictator Rashid Ali al-Gailani, as a pro-British government was re-established in Iraq. En route to Berlin, al-Husseini, together with al-Gailani, would stop in Tehran, Istanbul, and Rome, where al-Husseini met with the Fascist dictator Benito Mussolini on October 27, 1941. As was his custom wherever he resided, al-Husseini, an extremely rich man due to a lifetime of endowments from wealthy donors, stayed in a luxury hotel in Rome. Additionally, Mussolini granted him one million lira for expenses. Al-Husseini's memoirs record the following remarks made by Mussolini at their meeting:

> The number of Italian Jews is not more than forty-five thousand out of an Italian population of forty-five million . . . Each and every one of them is a spy and propagandist against us . . . therefore, our position in regard to them is the same as theirs to us . . . . If the Jews want it [a Jewish state], they should establish Tel Aviv in America . . . . They are our enemies . . . and there will be no place for them in Europe.

Upon his arrival in Berlin, on November 6, 1941, the Nazis set al-Husseini up as the de facto exiled führer of the Arabs, and in this capacity he was treated throughout the war as a visiting head of state. Al-Husseini would regularly negotiate by diplomatic pouch with Hitler, Mussolini, high-ranking Nazi officials, pro-Nazi governments, and Nazi functionaries. The Axis allies treated him with the type of pomp that would be normally afforded to an important visiting head of state and this royal treatment continued right into the very last days of the war. Al-Husseini would use his position in Nazi Germany to promote Nazi projects in Europe, to promote and further the aims of the Holocaust, and to promote a united Nazi-Arab *ummah* in the Arab world. Both al-Husseini and the Nazis discussed the grandiose and demented idea of establishing an axis between a united Nazi Europe and a united Nazi Middle East. Both al-Husseini and the Nazis hoped that such an axis would represent the ushering in of a new social order in the world, what the Nazis called the Thousand Year Reich.

While still in Rome and on his way to Berlin and the launching of his murderous career as an ally of Hitler, al-Husseini stated that in preparation for the establishment of their new social order, the Nazis and their Axis allies would have " . . . to settle the question of Jewish elements in Palestine and other Arab countries in accordance with the national and racial interests of the Arabs and along the lines similar to those used to solve the Jewish question in Germany and Italy."

Amin al-Husseini inspecting Nazi Muslim troops—1943

The Führer of the Arab World

Amin al-Husseini remained headquartered in Nazi Germany for three and one-half years, from November 1941 until the May 1945 end of the war. The Nazis gave him a luxurious mansion to live in, one that had been confiscated from a Jew, on the fashionable Klostock Street in what had been, until 1939, a Zionist-oriented Hebrew school. Al-Husseini referred to his new residence as "The Research Institute on the Jewish Problem in the Moslem World." al-Husseini was treated as a personal visiting guest of the Führer and was afforded the type of respect and prerogatives that are traditionally reserved for a visiting prime minister. Besides receiving a steady flow of funds from the *Sonderfund*, money confiscated from Jews on their way to concentration camps, al-Husseini was paid a stipend of over ten thousand dollars per month, which emanated directly from the Foreign Ministry, an exorbitant sum by the standards of the time.

Immediately upon his arrival in Nazi Germany, al-Husseini was publicly extolled at a reception given in his honor by the "Islamische Zentralinstitut," a Nazi-Islamic Institute. The reception was attended by fellow Muslim exiles and European Muslim leaders who honored al-Husseini with the title "Führer of the Arab World." In a speech at the

Nazi propaganda poster featuring Amin al-Husseini recruiting young Muslims.

reception, al-Husseini referred to the Jews as the "most fierce enemies of the Muslims" and an "ever corruptive element" in the world. While in Nazi Germany, al-Husseini would remain surrounded by a considerable entourage of Arab expatriates, many coming from prominent Palestinian Arab families. The Nazis set up a working bureau for the Arab expatriates in Berlin called the "Buro der Grossmufti."

At the famous, well-documented and photographed November 25, 1941 meeting in which Hitler received al-Husseini with all the pomp of a visiting head of state, Hitler promised him that he would be installed as führer over the entire Arab world once the Nazis crossed over the Caucasus Mountains and extended the Third Reich into the Middle East (*Appendix D*). Other issues discussed at this pivotal meeting involved a request by al-Husseini that Hitler publicly declare his support for the right of complete sovereignty for the Arab nations. Hitler demurred on this point, stating that such a declaration would have to be delayed so as not to offend his French and Italian allies, both of whom possessed colonies in the Arab world at the time. Both Hitler and al-Husseini agreed to set in motion a secret fomenting of pro-Nazi Arab revolts in the Middle East at a time to be determined by Hitler. Both agreed on the immediate setting up of pro-Nazi Arab legions to be made up of indigenous European Muslims trained in Europe, and both agreed on the final solution regarding the Jews of Palestine and the entire Arab world.

While there is no proof of this, it has been said that during the meeting and off the record, Hitler was reported to have broached al-Husseini with the idea of solving "the Jewish question" by deporting the Jews of Europe to Palestine. Al-Husseini was reported to have strenuously objected to this solution and instead pushed for what came to be known as "the final solution." Less than two months after the Hitler-al-Husseini meeting, January 20, 1942, at the Wannsee Conference, the Nazis officially established genocide as a state policy.

Amin al-Husseini in Berlin during World War II.

An April 28, 1942, formal letter, a written confirmation of certain aspects of the Hitler-al-Husseini meeting, was sent to both the "Grossmufti vom Jerusalem," as the Germans called al-Husseini, and the former Iraqi Prime Minister Rashid Ali al-Gailani, who also resided in Berlin. Al-Gailani, who was a rival to al-Husseini, was respected by the Germans as a regional Arab leader in a future Nazi-Arab Reich, but all indications point to the Germans viewing al-Gailani as subordinate to al-Husseini. The Italians at first considered al-Gailani as prime minister in exile until they also switched to al-Husseini in July 1942 after al-Husseini met with Italian Foreign Minister Count Galeazzo Ciano.

A letter co-authored by German Foreign Minister Joachim von Ribbentrop and Count Ciano would contain the declaration sought by al-Husseini, stating that Germany and Italy were prepared "to grant to the Arab countries in the Near East, now suffering under British oppression, every possible aid in their fight for liberation; to recognize their sovereignty and independence; to agree to their federation if this is desired by the interested parties; as well as to the abolition of the Jewish National Homeland in Palestine." al-Husseini claimed that this letter constituted a formal recognition by Nazi Germany and Italy of a united Arab *ummah*, the promise of aid in the attainment of this goal, and their assistance in his plan to liquidate the Jews in Palestine. This letter came at a critical period for the Axis powers as the Allied forces, commanded by American General Dwight D. Eisenhower, had landed in North Africa and were advancing toward Tunis.

Al-Husseini responded to the letter by fulfilling his part of the bargain as he ratcheted up his pro-Nazi activities involving the spreading of pro-Nazi propaganda, espionage, sabotage, and a general attempt to foment revolt in the Arab world. At this time, al-Husseini was put in charge of recruiting Bosnian and Albanian Muslims in Nazi-occupied Yugoslavia and Muslims in occupied Russia into what came to be known as the Hanzar brigades, as well as other formations. In May 1942, al-Husseini also began a series of regular radio broadcasts to the Arab world, which were carried on Bari radio. The Bari station was equipped with a powerful transmitter, and Bari is located on the southern tip of Italy, within listening range of a large segment of the Arab world.

In one of his radio addresses, al-Husseini used the execution, by the pro-British government in Iraq, of two of the members of the pro-Nazi Golden Square generals who were involved in the 1941 coup as an excuse for propaganda against the British. In one of his more infamous broadcasts, beamed into the Arab world from several transmitters that would receive the signal from Bari, al-Husseini, in typical fashion, declared: "Oh Arabs, use and avenge your martyrs. Avenge your honor. Fight for your independence. I, mufti of Palestine, declare this war as a holy war against the British yoke of injustice, indecency, and tyranny. We fear not death, if in death there is life and liberty." While these broadcasts, along with propaganda pamphlets and acts of sabotage, ultimately failed to trigger any discernable revolt in the Arab world, their message continues to incite over fifty years after the collapse of the Thousand Year Reich.

Al-Husseini conducted a broadcast in Arabic from Berlin immediately after the 1942 Allied victory against the Nazi forces of Field Marshall Erwin Rommel at El Alamein, Egypt, the first significant setback in al-Husseini's dark plans for the Middle East. In this bone-chilling broadcast, al-Husseini implored the Arabs to not lose sight of what he said would be the inevitable victory of the Third Reich in North Africa and the establishment of Nazi-Muslim hegemony. Even though the triumphal conquest of Palestine by the Nazis had been temporarily set back due to Allied victories, al-Husseini strenuously asserted in his broadcast that he, nevertheless, planned a grand return at the vanguard of a Nazi-Muslim army and that he planned to set up a concentration camp for the Jews outside of Nablus. The famous quote from this broadcast is:

"Arise, o sons of Arabia, fight for your sacred rights. Slaughter Jews wherever you find them. Their spilled blood pleases Allah, our history and religion. That will save our honor."

Al-Husseini also broadcast into Nazi-occupied Russia, where he exhorted native Muslims, including Crimean Tartars and Chechens, to join forces with the occupying Nazis and to prepare themselves for the "liberation" of their Arab homeland. Scores of Muslims, native to the region, responded to al-Husseini's pleas by joining the various Nazi and Nazi-sponsored military units, including the infamous Nazi mobile genocide brigades known as the Einsatzgruppen. In these broadcasts, al-Husseini referred to these Eastern European Muslim soldiers as the "cream of Islam." In all of his communications, al-Husseini was careful to associate Nazism with Islam, and often in intricate detail, as he expressed solidarity between the two movements. There is no reason to assume that al-Husseini was anything but utterly sincere in this belief, a belief that continues to reverberate.

Al-Husseini's operations, both within the Third Reich and in the Middle East, were funded primarily from what was known as the *Sonderfund*, which consisted of capital and property that had been confiscated from Jewish families before they were transferred to concentration camps and crematoria. Besides covering expenses for propaganda, sabotage, and espionage in the Arab world, not to mention the maintenance of the same lavish lifestyle he enjoyed all his life, al-Husseini used this *Sonderfund* to pay off friends and allies, to help form and maintain Nazi-Muslim militias such as the Hanzar brigades, and to lavishly finance the Islamische Zentralinstitut, the Islamic Institute, in Dresden, and the Goettingen School for Muslims, which served as training grounds for Muslim-Nazi troops and for future Nazi-Muslim leaders. The question of where these thousands of Nazi-Muslim graduates of these schools ended up is an intriguing one that should be the subject of an intensive investigation.

In the last months of the war, Berlin was under heavy and almost daily bombardment and al-Husseini's house was at one point hit by an Allied bomb. In the midst of terrible defeat and depredation, the Nazi foreign office somehow continued to maintain al-Husseini in the comfort which he had been accustomed, which is proof of how valuable he was to Hitler. In April 1945, in the final weeks and days of the war, al-Husseini, after having refused an offer by the Nazi Foreign Ministry to provide him with a private plane trip to Switzerland, bought a car and drove himself to the Swiss border. He was refused entry into Switzerland and was instead arrested by the French occupying force and transferred to a sub-urb of Paris where he was placed under house arrest.

Curiously, the French were careful to insure that al-Husseini was taken care of during his internment in a private French chateau, where he was provided luxuries such as a Tunisian cook. Al-Husseini would not stay in Paris long, as he was made aware of written testimony being given to the Nuremberg investigators by Adolf Eichmann's assistant, Hermann Krumey, regarding his participation in the extermination of the Hungarian Jews. Rumors were also circulating at the time concerning an impending indictment of al-Husseini from Yugoslavia for crimes against humanity for his role in the Hanzar genocide against the Serbs. After securing an invitation to settle in Egypt from King Farouk, al-Husseini fled Paris on May 29, 1945, one step ahead of a likely indictment as a war criminal at Nuremberg. Hence, the true role of al-Husseini regarding his involve-ment in these heinous crimes would never be investigated, he would remain for the rest of his life beyond the reach of justice, and most of the evidence against him shall most likely remain lost in the mists of history.

Amin al-Husseini inspects his Muslim-Nazi Hanzar troops—1943.

The Grand Mufti and the Holocaust

Amin al-Husseini was a significant and, indeed, key player in the Holocaust against the Jews. The fact that his role is virtually ignored by researchers and scholars of the Holocaust is curious indeed. A most notorious example of the level of involvement of al-Husseini in the Holocaust, one that is well documented with a letter in al-Husseini's own handwriting, occurred in 1942, when Red Cross officials offered to mediate in an exchange with the Nazis of 4,000 orphaned Polish Jewish children who had been separated from their parents and 500 Jewish adults. The Jews were to be sent to Palestine in exchange for the return to Germany of pro-Nazi Templar Germans who had settled in Palestine around the turn of the century. Adolf Eichmann, who was in charge of such matters, was considering agreeing to the transfer until he read the letter from al-Husseini, dated May 13, 1942, and addressed to von Ribbentrop and forwarded to him, objecting to the transfer. In the letter, al-Husseini was reported to have said something to the effect that little Jews will grow up to be big Jews. The 4,000 Jewish children and 500 Jewish adults were instead sent to Auschwitz. The Jewish Agency for Palestine presented an authenticated copy of this letter to the British on February 26, 1946, in an unsuccessful attempt to see that al-Husseini was charged with war crimes.

On June 28, 1943, al-Husseini, acting in his capacity as the head of state of the Nazi-Muslim government-in-exile, wrote to the pro-Nazi foreign minister of Romania and was successful in his attempt to stop Romania from agreeing to allow 1,800 Jewish children and 200 Jewish adults to leave Romania and to emigrate to Palestine. On the same day, he also wrote to the pro-Nazi foreign minister of Hungary regarding the possible immigration of 900 Jewish children and 100 Jewish adults seeking passage to Palestine. In the letter to Hungary, al-Husseini suggested that the Hungarian government would be better served by sending their Jews where they would be "under active supervision, for example in Poland" (*Appendix E*).

These letters went a long way toward convincing these governments to send their Jewish children and adults to the Nazi concentration camps. By any estimation, these letters served to tip the balance in favor of the rounding up and concentrating of Jews into transit camps. Subsequently, the Jews of Romania and Hungary were put on boxcars and sent to the death camps. Al-Husseini sent these letters at a time when the Holocaust against the Jews was at its height of operation.

In the letter to the Hungarian foreign minister, published in the appendix of this book, al-Husseini pitches to him a dark conspiratorial view of a Jewish Palestine, one that was widely disseminated by the Nazis. The conspiracy theory proffered is of a secret cabal of powerful Jews conspiring to create a Jewish state in Palestine for the express purpose of establishing a centrally located foothold and a launching pad for world conquest.

Whether al-Husseini actually believed this demented theory or not is beside the point, as the evidence suggests that he was one of its chief proponents and promoters. Al-Husseini was a major promoter of this theory and other lethal libels regarding Jews and Israel in the Arab world, where these lies retain a considerable degree of cachet today and are articles of faith to many.

The Nazis were employing the classic ploy of scapegoating. The Jews were blamed for what the Nazis themselves were obviously engaged in, which was a literal campaign of world subjagation, an undisputed fact that requires for proof nothing more than a simple observation of events surrounding World War II. It was the Nazis themselves who operated as a small cabal of sinister men and who used Germany as a launching pad for their own diabolical world designs.

The Nazis, and also the Communists, in fact constituted vast conspiracies that did, in fact, plot to conquer the world. Nazism and Communism were imperialistic world order movements while Zionism was, is, and will forevermore remain a strictly nationalist movement calling for the establishment of Jewish sovereignty in that tiny piece of turf known then as Palestine. Zionism is the national movement for independence for the Jewish people in Palestine, only Palestine, and nothing but Palestine. Today, the followers of al-Husseini seek to turn the tables on Israel in a similar manner to the Nazis by claiming that Israel is "Nazi" while diverting attention from their own history, beliefs, and aspirations. The indisputable and acknowledged fact is that the radical Islamists still have pan-Arab ambitions, and many of them are still plotting and carrying out genocide against the Jews of Israel, as evidenced by the suicide bombers, the many mass-murdering terrorist acts, and the attempted missile assault of an El Al flight leaving Mombassa Airport in Kenya.

Al-Husseini wrote a terse letter to Nazi Foreign Minister von Ribbentrop, dated July 25, 1944, in which he complained about Jews having been exchanged on July 2, 1944, against his previous direct request. In this scolding and imperious letter, al-Husseini reminded von Ribbentrop of a public declaration of Nazi policy going back to November 2, 1943, that promised to destroy the Jewish National Home in Palestine and to "battle against world Jewry" (*den Kampf gegen das Weltjudentum*).

Rudolf Kastner, the representative of the Jewish Rescue and Relief Committee in Budapest who would himself be tried in Israel in the early 1950s for collaborating with the Nazis, contacted his close friend Adolf Eichmann, requesting that the Hungarian Jews be allowed to emigrate to Palestine, rather than putting them on the boxcars to Poland. According to Kastner, Eichmann responded to the request by saying, "I am a personal friend of the Grand Mufti. We have promised him that no European Jew would enter Palestine anymore," and that he (Eichmann) "would be willing to recommend the emigration of a group of 1,681 Hungarian Jews on condition that the group not go to Palestine. They may get to any country but Palestine." This statement was made with the full knowledge that all doors had been slammed shut to the Jews.

SS chief Heinrich Himmler seemed to have taken al-Husseini under his wing, as the many written correspondences between them attest.

Besides charging al-Husseini with organizing Nazi-Muslim brigades, Himmler arranged for al-Husseini to regularly tour Auschwitz, where al-Husseini could make sure the death camp was operating efficiently. Himmler also took a great interest in and helped finance al-Husseini's clerical academies, particularly in Dresden, where future Nazi-Muslim leaders were receiving their education and training.

Amin al-Husseini meets Heinrich Himmler, head of Nazi SS.

Toward the end of the war, al-Husseini seemed to have ratcheted up his activities to a hysterical pitch, as is indicated by his radio broadcasts. On November 11, 1943, broadcasting on Radio Bari, al-Husseini called for Arabs to fight America, Britain, and the Jews when he stated, "If America and England win the war, the Jews will dominate the world."

On March 1, 1944, al-Husseini attacked America in a radio broadcast from Berlin:

> "No one ever thought that 140,000 Americans would become tools in Jewish hands. How would the Americans dare to Judaize Palestine? The wicked American intentions towards the Arabs are now clear, and there remain no doubts that they are endeavoring to establish a Jewish empire in the Arab world."

On March 4, 1944, al-Husseini delivered a speech from Berlin where he exhorted the Muslim Hanzar SS troops, to whom he referred in the broadcast as the "cream of Islam," to "kill the Jews wherever you find them." He also asserted that "This pleases Allah, History, and Religion, Allah is with you." One Nazi officer in attendance noted in his journal that al-Husseini wanted to see the Jews "preferably all killed." On a visit to Auschwitz, he was reported to have admonished the guards running the gas chambers to work more diligently. A document was presented to the U.N. in 1947, which contained al-Husseini's June 28, 1943, letter to the Hungarian foreign minister requesting the deportation of Hungarian Jews to Poland (*Appendix F*). This document contained the following notation: "As a Sequel to This Request 400,000 Jews Were Subsequently Killed."

In postwar testimony at Nuremberg, Dieter Wisliceny, Adolf Eichmann's deputy, who would himself be convicted of war crimes and executed by the Allies, stated, "The mufti was one of the initiators of the systematic extermination of European Jewry and had been a collaborator and advisor of Eichmann and Himmler in the execution of this plan . . . . He was one of Eichmann's best friends and had constantly incited him to accelerate the extermination measures. I heard him say, accompanied by Eichmann, he had visited incognito the gas chamber of Auschwitz." Wisliceny testified that al-Husseini had chastised the Auschwitz authorities for not being efficient enough in their work.

Al-Husseini wrote about his meeting with Hitler in his own diary (*Appendix F*). Long after the fact, he presented his reasoning behind his support of the Nazis and the purpose of his mission in Germany when he stated, "the objectives of my fight are clear. Primarily, I am fighting the Jews without respite, and this fight includes the fight against the so-called Jewish National Home in Palestine." His stated reasons for opposing a Jewish Palestine dovetail with the bizarre conspiracy theories both he and the Nazis embraced at the time, theories that led them to justify the Holocaust in their own minds. He stated that he opposed a Jewish Palestine because "the Jews want to establish there a central government for their own pernicious purposes, and to undertake a devastating and ruinous expansion at the expense of the governments of the world and of other peoples." Never mind the fact that what al-Husseini was describing was exactly the intent and policy of Hitler himself and that of the Nazis, and for that matter, of al-Husseini himself and the Islamic extremists.

Amin al-Husseini at a Nazi meeting in Berlin during WW II.

In the same diary excerpt as his meeting with Hitler, al-Husseini, in his own hand, wrote, "I am resolved to find a solution for the Jewish problem, progressing step by step without cessation. With regard to this I am making the necessary and right appeal, first to all the European countries and then to countries outside of Europe." This was the appeal al-Husseini made to Hitler two months before the Wannsee conference. This was the appeal al-Husseini made to pro-Nazi countries suggesting that they send their Jews to the concentration camps (*Appendix F*). He regularly appealed to Arabs in his broadcasts to "kill the Jews wherever you find them."

In his diary, al-Husseini espoused a bizarre conspiracy theory regarding a "hidden Jewry" that, he alleged, was secretly controlling "Great Britain and the Soviets whose principles are opposed to ours." He wrote of a "life and death struggle" that would "not only determine the outcome of the struggle between National Socialism and Jewry, but also of the Arabs who are engaged in the same struggle."

The Nazis saw the Jews as the main obstacle in their own conspiracy to create a "new social order" in a utopian world. Likewise, the Communists saw the bourgeoisie as standing in the path of their conspiracy toward world conquest. Today, the radical Islamists, largely due to the influence of al-Husseini, have continued the old Nazi conspiracy theory that the Jews are the main culprits standing in their path to a utopian Dar el-Islam while they blow up buildings filled with "infidels."

It should be noted that one of the most central tenets of Judaism, the message Jews are taught that God delivered to the Israelites at Sinai through their Prophet Moses, was that the mission of the Israelites was not to control nations or peoples, but rather to simply serve the Almighty in ways that are delineated in the Torah. The only land that the Almighty, blessed be He, commanded the Jews to take dominion over was that tiny and inscrutable piece of sod that is Israel and nowhere else. The borders of the Holy Land are clearly and unequivocally demarked in intricate detail in the Torah and they are the land between the river (Jordan) to the east and the sea (Mediterranean) to the west, Dan (Mt. Hermon) to the north and Beersheba to the south. While the ancient Israelites occupied other lands from time to time, only the aforementioned is the land that the Almighty promised Abraham, Isaac, and Jacob. Modern Israel exists today within these exact and modest Biblical parameters. The only area in which Israel exists outside of the Holy Land is an insignificant swath of unwanted desert wasteland called the Negev, which lies due south of the ancient city of Beersheba.

Al-Husseini maintained his headquarters in Nazi Germany waiting for Hitler to install him as the führer of the Arabs after the Nazi "new social order" established itself in a conquered and subdued Europe. He made it clear to Hitler that he supported the extermination of the Jews of Europe and that he expected Hitler to help in exterminating the Jews of Palestine and of the Arab world. It is reasonable to assume that a primary motive of both al-Husseini and Hitler for recruiting Nazi-Muslim brigades was to use them as shock troops for an invasion and occupation of the Arab countries. In the Balkans, the Nazi-Muslim brigades, who considered al-Husseini their leader, directly participated in genocide against Serbs, Jews, and Roma. From his post as head of a Nazi-Muslim government-in-exile, al-Husseini strove mightily to incite rebellion in the Arab world with incendiary broadcasts, financial support, sabotage, and espionage. Al-Husseini was a fully witting and conscious participant in the Holocaust against the Jews of Europe and probably played a more extensive role than will ever be known.

Al-Husseini was directly responsible for convincing the Nazis, as well as pro-Nazi governments in Hungary, Romania, and Bulgaria, to send their Jews to the death camps rather than to allow them immigrate to Palestine. These actions alone directly place the responsibility

for the murder of hundreds of thousands of European Jews directly onto the shoulders of al-Husseini. His influence as a consultant on "the Jewish question" to the Nazis and the overall force of his mission greatly contributed to the genocidal program.

It is entirely reasonable to suggest that the juxtaposition of the Hitler-al-Husseini meeting and the decision soon after to liquidate European Jewry indicate that al-Husseini, with all that is known about his hatred of Jews, was directly and decisively involved in that decision. It is a reasonable assertion, in light of all that is known, that the entire motivation for al-Husseini to ally himself to Hitler and to reside in Germany during World War II was to ensure that the Jews of Europe were annihilated, with the fervent hope that the annihilation would then extend to the Arab world and eventually to the entire world.

In his own memoirs, al-Husseini wrote: "Our fundamental condition for cooperating with Germany was a free hand to eradicate every last Jew from Palestine and the Arab world. I asked Hitler for an explicit undertaking to allow us to solve the Jewish problem in a manner befitting our national and racial aspirations and according to the scientific methods innovated by Germany in the handling of its Jews. The answer I got was: 'The Jews are yours.'"

The Hanzar Brigades

Exclusively Muslim military formations had been introduced into Christian Europe in the early twentieth century by the Austro-Hungarians after their annexation of Bosnia-Herzegovina from the Ottoman Turks. There were large areas of the Balkans, especially the area centered around Albania and Bosnia-Herzegovina, where populations had converted to Islam after having lived for centuries under Turkish rule. Turkey ruled the area quite harshly for hundreds of years and Christians were often prosecuted with special taxes, or what was known as the *jizya*; *dhimmi* status, or second-class citizenship; forced conscription into the military; and the occasional massacre of a Christian village. While the Serbs largely remained fiercely loyal to their church and paid a brutal price for doing so, many others in the Turkish-occupied Balkans took the path of least resistance and converted.

The Muslim brigades established by the newly arriving Austrians proved to be fierce and ruthless fighters and were thus given special privileges by the Austrian army. Immediately after the Nazi occupation of the Balkans in 1941, a Nazi-Muslim unit was established called the Deutsch-Arabische Lehr Abteilung (DAL), which immediately began operations in Nazi-occupied Greece. Al-Husseini referred to the DAL

Amin al-Husseini with one of his Nazi-Muslim troops—1943 Hanzar SS Division.

as the "Arab liberation force," and the unit would later be transferred to the Russian front in the summer of 1942 in anticipation of crossing the Caucasus and conquering the motherland from the British. The unit wore the inscription "Free Arabia" on their sleeves.

Shortly after his November 25, 1941, meeting with Hitler, al-Husseini met with Gottlob Berger, the chief recruiter for the elite Schutzstaffel SS. This meeting was followed by a meeting between al-Husseini and SS Reichsführer Heinrich Himmler. Himmler, who subsequently maintained regular contact and correspondence with al-Husseini, proceeded to place al-Husseini in charge of the recruiting of Muslims into elite units to serve in the Nazi-occupied Balkans, Russia, North Africa, and the Middle East. Waffen-SS Nazi-Muslim divisions were established, as well as Muslim units serving directly under the command of the Nazi Wehrmacht. Berger stated at the time that "a link is created between Islam and National-Socialism on an open, honest basis. It will be directed in terms of blood and race from the North, and in the ideological-spiritual sphere from the East." Clearly Berger was one Nazi, one among many, who understood the ideological and spiritual symbiosis between Nazism and a radicalized Islam.

Approximately 100,000 European Muslims were recruited and fought for Nazi Germany during the course of the war. This astonishing fact of history is recorded as barely a footnote in the published history of the war. Distinctly Nazi-Muslim divisions and formations were developed, including two Bosnian Muslim Waffen-SS Divisions, an Albanian Waffen-SS Division in Kosovo and Western Macedonia, the Twenty-First Waffen-Gebirgs Division der SS Skanderbeg, a Muslim SS self-defense regiment in the Muslim Rashka region of Serbia, the Arab Legion (Arabisches Freiheitskorps), the Arab Brigade, the Ostmusselmanische SS-Regiment, the Ostturkischen Waffen-Verband der SS made up of Turkistanis, the Waffen-Gruppe der-SS Krim, formations consisting of Chechen Muslims from Chechnya, a Tatar Regiment der-SS made up of Crimean Tatars, and other Muslim formations in Bosnia-Herzegovina, elsewhere in the Balkans, and in other Nazi-occupied areas of the Soviet Union and North Africa.[2]

Following the April 1941 Nazi conquest and occupation of Yugoslavia, on April 10, 1941, the Nazis established a puppet state in Croatia. Besides recognition by Nazi Germany, Nazi-Croatia would be recognized only by Italian dictator Benito Mussolini and by the Vatican. Croatia operated as a full partner in the Axis and was placed under the control of the infamous pro-Nazi Ustasha party. The Croatian-Nazi

Muslim Soldiers reading German propaganda. The name of the book is Islam Und Judentum *(Islam and Judaism in German).*

regime was made up of an alliance between Catholics and Muslims as Ante Pavelic, a Catholic, would be president and Dzafer Kulenovic, a Bosnian Muslim, would be vice president. Croatia would come to practice a most extreme form of fascism.

Upon taking power, the Croatian Ustacha party, and its militia wing, would immediately launch a genocidal program against the Christian Orthodox Serb, Roma, and Jewish minorities. Bosnian Muslims made up a significant component of the Ustacha as Bosnia-Herzegovina was a semi-autonomous subsection of the greater Nazi-Croatia. As proof of the Muslim element in the Ustacha, SS chief recruiter Gottlob Berger issued a direct order to the Ustacha in 1943 to release all Muslim troops to al-Husseini and the newly formed Bosnian Hanzar brigades. A Nazi-Croat-Muslim party, the Young Muslims (Mladi Muslimani), included as a member a young Alija Izetbegovic, who would later become president of the Bosnian-Muslim government in the 1990s.[3] Muslim participation in the activities of the brutal Croatian Ustacha death squads and infantry divisions was extensive. Many Croatian Muslims lobbied the Nazis for additional autonomy for Bosnia.

Croatian leader Mile Budak described the Croatian plan of genocide on July 22, 1941: "The basis for the Ustasha movement is religion. For minorities such as Serbs, Jews, and Gypsies, we have three million bullets." On July 6, 1941, Budak defined the Bosnian Muslim role in Croatia: "The Croatian state is Christian. It is also a Moslem state where our people are of the Mohammedan religion." The Croatians of post-1990 Yugoslavia have resurrected certain aspects of this unholy

Amin al-Hussseini meets Croat Nazis A. Artukovic and M. Budak.

alliance between Catholics and Muslims in parts of Bosnia and in the massive ethnic cleansing operations against Serbs in Bosnia and Croatia. The Croatian Nazis murdered approximately 200,000 Serbs, 40,000 Gypsies, and 22,000 Jews by the end of the war.

In an attempt to improve levels of Muslim recruitment into the SS as well as to reestablish the old Austro-Hungarian system of special and elite Muslim military units that were traditionally granted special privileges, Heinrich Himmler decided to back semi-autonomy for Bosnia-Herzegovina. Himmler stated, "I decided to propose to the Führer that we establish a Muslim Bosnian Division. Many believed the notion to be so novel that they scoffed at it. Such is the fate of all new ideas. I was told, you're ruining the formation of the Croatian state and no one will volunteer. Germany and the Reich have been friends of Islam for two centuries, owing not to expediency but to friendly conviction. We have the same goals."

Himmler, over the objection of the Nazi-Croatian puppet dictator Ante Pavelic, arranged for the creation of a semi-autonomous Muslim Bosnia within Croatia and sent al-Husseini to Sarajevo to begin recruiting for the Thirteenth Waffen-SS Hanzar and other Muslim divisions such as the Kama division. Al-Husseini had already publicly stated his intention to form an "Arab Brigade" in response to the establishment of the "Jewish Brigade" by the British in Palestine.

The Hanzars, named for a dagger traditionally carried on the belt of Ottoman Turkish officers, would subsequently grow to about twenty-two thousand men and would become the third-largest unit of the

Bosnian Nazi Muslim flag under Amin al-Husseini—1943.

Waffen-SS. On February 10, 1943, the Hanzars, with al-Husseini acting as an advisor and deriving his authority from Hitler and Himmler,
received a direct order to deport the Bosnian Serbs and the Roma, and
to transfer the Bosnian and Croatian Jews to Auschwitz. The largest
concentration camp and transfer station in Bosnia was the Kruscica
camp near Travnik, which had been established April-May, 1941. The
Nazi-Muslim brigades did a lion's share of the dirty work, particularly
in Bosnia, in terms of ethnic cleansing and deportations.

By the summer of 1944, the Hanzars had literally taken de facto control of eastern and northern sections of Bosnia, where they exercised
carte blanche as they slaughtered Serbs and wiped out Serbian villages.
Perhaps some of the tough Serbian response to a Muslim-controlled
Bosnia in the 1990s was a result of the crimes committed against the
Serbian minority of Bosnia in those years. It should also be pointed out
that Serbia, even while under a brutal Nazi occupation, protected its
minorities, including its Jews.

In 1943, the Serbian Eastern Orthodox Diocese of the U.S. and Canada
reported on the actions of the Bosnian Muslims in the Ustasha before the
formation of the Bosnian Muslim Hanzar brigades. The report stated,
"The behavior of the Muslims was traditionally treacherous. As always,
they were in the camp of those who were momentarily in power. More
than ninety-five percent of Muslims joined the Ustashi and participated
very actively in the massacre of the Serbs, as, for instance, in the city of
Mostar, where great numbers of killings were done personally by
Huremovich, a Muslim. The Ustasha terror began in Mostar. The Ustashi,
the majority of them local Mohammedans, are arresting, looting, and
shipping off Serbs or killing them and throwing their bodies in the Neretva
River. They are throwing Serbs alive into chasms and are burning whole
families locked in their homes. Outside of Zagreb, the strongest Ustasha
hotbed is Sarajevo. The Muslims committed unbelievable barbarities for
they murdered women and children, even with scissors."

The Hanzars were sworn to service with an oath to the Third Reich,
composed by Heinrich Himmler, that read as follows: "I swear to the
Führer, Adolf Hitler, as Supreme Commander of the German Armed
Forces, to be loyal and brave. I swear to the Führer and to the leaders
whom he may designate, obedience unto death."

Himmler expressed his view of Islam in a letter to Joseph Goebbels:
"I have nothing against Islam because it educates the men in this division

for me and promises them heaven if they fight and are killed in action. A very practical and attractive religion for soldiers." No doubt, Himmler's attitude toward Islam was shared by Nazi elites and reveals an intimate understanding by the Nazis of the similarities between aspects of a radicalized Islam and Nazism.

In an August 6, 1943, letter to Croatian and Waffen-SS field commanders, Himmler, who was on record as admiring the "natural alliance that exists between the National-Socialism of Great Germany and the freedom-loving Muslims of the world," established official policy regarding Muslim recruits:

> "All Moslem members of the Waffen-SS and police are to be afforded the undeniable right of their religious demands never to touch pork, pork sausages nor to drink alcohol . . . I hold all commanders . . . and other SS officers, responsible for the most scrupulous and loyal respect for this privilege especially granted to the Moslems. They have answered the call of the Moslem chiefs and have come to us out of hatred for the common Jewish-Anglo-Bolshevik enemy and through respect and fidelity for he who they respect above all, the Führer, Adolf Hitler . . . .There will no longer be the least discussion about the special rights afforded to the Moslems in these circles.
>
> Heil Hitler
> (signed) H. Himmler

On November 22, 1943, Himmler wrote to al-Husseini, who was attending what apparently was an annual Nazi-sponsored anti-Balfour Declaration meeting. In the letter, found in the archives of the postwar Arab Higher Committee, Himmler stated:

> "The National Socialist movement of Greater Germany has, since its beginning, inscribed upon its flag the fight against world Jewry. It has therefore, followed with particular sympathy the struggle of the freedom-loving Arabians, especially in Palestine, against the Jewish interlopers. It is in recognition of this enemy and of the common struggle against him that lies the firm foundation of the natural alliance that exists between National Socialist Greater Germany and the freedom-loving Moslems of the whole world."

In January 1944, al-Husseini spent three days visiting Hanzar soldiers preparing to depart from Germany to Bosnia by rail. Al-Husseini's
speech that day to the division sheds a great deal of light on his philosophy and worldview:

"This division of Bosnian Muslims established with the help of
Greater Germany, is an example to Muslims in all countries. There
is no other deliverance for them from imperialistic oppression than
hard fighting to preserve their homes and faith. Many common interests exist between the Islamic world and Greater Germany, and those
make cooperation a matter of course. The Reich is fighting against
the same enemies who robbed the Muslims of their countries and
suppressed their faith in Asia, Africa, and Europe . . . "

"Germany is the only Great Power, which has never attacked any Islamic country. Further, National-Socialist Germany is fighting against
world Jewry. The Koran says: you will find that the Jews are the worst
enemies of the Muslims. There are also considerable similarities
between Islamic principles and those of National Socialism, namely in
the affirmation of struggle and fellowship, in stressing leadership, in the
idea of order, in the high valuation of work. All this brings our ideologies close together and facilitates cooperation. I am happy to see in this
division a visible and practical expression of both ideologies."

Al-Husseini spoke to Nazi-Muslim imams also departing the Islamic
Nazi institutes for Bosnia with the Hanzars at which time he referred to
the Bosnian Muslims as the cream of Islam:

"Friendship and collaboration between two peoples must be built on
a firm foundation. The necessary ingredients here are common spiritual and material interests as well as the same ideals. The relationship
between the Muslims and the Germans is built on this foundation.
Never in its history has Germany attacked a Muslim nation. Germany battles world Jewry, Islam's principal enemy. Germany also battles England and its allies, who have persecuted millions of Muslims,
as well as Bolshevism, which subjugates forty million Muslims and
threatens the Islamic faith in other lands. Any one of these arguments
would be enough of a foundation for a friendly relationship between

two peoples. My enemy's enemy is my friend . . . you, my Bosnian Muslims, are the first Islamic division, and serve as an example of the active collaboration between Germany and the Muslims. I wish you much success in your holy mission."

The view of al-Husseini, along with those of the Nazi-Muslim imams, was that the Balkan Muslims were to view themselves as spiritually Arab but racially Germanic. According to crackpot Nazi race mythology, the Balkan Muslims were of Gothic, rather than of Slavic, descent, which placed them a step over the Slavs on the Nazi pecking order.

Nazi Imam Abdullah Muhasilovic delivered a speech to the departing Hanzars, which captures the view of the mufti and the Nazi-Muslims:

"The world's Muslims are engaged in a terrible life-or-death struggle. Today, a war of enormous magnitude is being waged; a war as humanity has never before experienced. The entire world has divided itself into two camps. One stands under the leadership of the Jews. About whom Allah says in the Koran, They are your enemy and Allah's enemy. And that is the English, Americans, and Bolsheviks, who fight against faith, against Allah, against morality, and a just order . . . on the other side stands National Socialist Germany with its allies, under the leadership of Adolf Hitler, who fight for Allah, faith, morality, and a fairer and more righteous order in the world, as well as for a fairer distribution of all goods that Allah has produced for all people."

Nazi Imam Dzozo said of the Bosnian Muslim SS soldier:

"Bosnia's best sons are serving in the SS. After victory is achieved, a new, important task must be completed—the implementation of the New Order. Through the Versailles-Diktat, Europe was thrust into a totally senseless foundation, and under the name of democracy, Jews and Freemasons played key roles in political and societal life. It will not be easy to liberate Europe from these enemies, but the SS man shall build a better future for Europe."

In 1944, al-Husseini approved of a plan that had been presented to him by the Albanian Nazi-Muslim leader Bedri Pajani that would have

Bosnian soldier posting picture of Amin al-Husseini—1943.

created a greater pan-Muslim state for Albania that was to include Kosovo, western Macedonia, southern Montenegro, portions of Bosnia, and the Rashka region of Serbia. While the Nazis, overextended and in retreat in the face of Allied advances at the time, rejected this idea, a variation of this al-Husseini-approved Pajani Plan for Greater Albania has actually been resurrected like an old apparition as it haunts the region today.

After the war, the image and crimes of the Hanzar brigades and other Muslim military formations, specifically the Hanzar role in the genocide against the Serbs, would be largely sanitized and air-brushed out of history by the newly arriving Communist regime of Marshal Josip Broz Tito, who sought to curry favor with the Arab world. Tito would instead portray the Bosnian Muslims as the victims rather than as the perpetrators of the genocide that they had in fact initiated against Serbs, Roma, and Jews. The many respected and well-documented histories of World War II and the Holocaust have also, for some strange reason, fallen short in terms of researching or even mentioning anything about the Hanzars.[1]

Nazi officer inspecting Muslim Bosnian SS troops.

Amin al-Husseini inspecting his Nazi-Muslim troops-1943.

In the mid-1990s, after the breakaway of Bosnia from Yugoslavia and the subsequent disintegration of the multiethnic Bosnia into three distinct ethnic enclaves, the Muslim Hanzars made a comeback in the Muslim sector. Reporter Robert Fox, in a *Daily Telegraph* article entitled "Albanians and Afghans Fight for Heirs of Bosnia's SS," quotes a Hanzar fighter telling a U.N. officer, "We do everything with the knife, and we always fight on the frontline." This was in reference to the murder and ethnic cleansing of at least half of the Serbian-Bosnian town of Fojnica, a town of approximately 15,000.[2]

The new Hanzar brigades, at about 6,000 strong at the time the article was published in 1993, openly identifies with the Nazi SS Hanzar brigades of the Nazi past and looks with nostalgia to the grand mufti, Haj Amin al-Husseini, as their spiritual mentor. U.N. sources say that today's Hanzar brigade is trained and led by veteran mujahideen fighters from Afghanistan and Pakistan. The majority of the soldiers in the brigade do not speak Serbo-Croatian, but are instead of Albanian background and come from either Albania or Kosovo. It is considered likely that bin Laden's Al Qaeda has supplied experts and arms and maintains contacts within the Hanzars. Additionally, the Hanzars are known to enjoy considerable support from the Bosnian Muslim government and military.

In one of their first acts, a four-man Hanzar death squad murdered

Muslim soldiers with hats showing Nazi insignia—WW II.

Muslim Nazi troops in traditional Muslim prayer—1943.

two Serbian monks in a monastery in the village of Fojnica. After an argument with the squad, Brother Nikola Milicevic, thirty-nine, was shot dead on the spot and Brother Mato Migic, fifty-six, was wounded and then finished off with a bullet in the neck. The clerical Provincial for the Franciscans of Bosnia, Petar Andjelovic, demanded an explanation for the atrocity from the Bosnian Muslim government. He received perfunctory condolences from Bosnian President Alija Izetbegovic, himself a protégé of al-Husseini and a former member of the pro-Nazi-Muslim Young Muslims (Mladi Muslimani) as a young man. The killing of Christians who refuse to submit, a reoccurring theme in Muslim-controlled parts of the Balkans, seems to be making a comeback in the region.

The Death of the Grand Mufti

Amin al-Husseini, while still in Nazi Germany, played a significant role in founding the Arab League in 1944. Given the fact that al-Husseini, while backed by funds emanating from the *Sonderfund*, was a leader in the recruitment of Nazi-Muslims into the Hanzar brigades and other Nazi-Muslim formations, and that one of the earliest of those formations was called the "Arabisches Freiheitskorps," or the Arab Brigade, it is not by any means inconceivable and actually quite plausible that the Arab League itself was organized with financing from the *Sonderfund* and even was possibly secretly organized in Nazi Germany. During his famous meeting with Hitler, al-Husseini and Hitler discussed the issue of forming an Arab Legion (*Appendix D*). The Arab League would, at any rate, come to embody and personify, in the post–World War II period, the merger of the ideology of Nazism and Islamic precepts of pan-Arabism.

In late 1944, in the last monstrous months of Hitler's war, al-Husseini attempted a final desperate move to trigger a pro-Nazi Arab rebellion and to kill the Jews of Palestine. Al-Husseini arranged for a Nazi-Arab commando unit to parachute into Palestine with the goal of poisoning the water wells of Tel Aviv.[1] Amazingly the British, after all that transpired, would grant al-Husseini a full amnesty after the war in spite of their full knowledge of his record of Nazi collaboration. This shameful and inexplicable act of appeasement constituted yet another move by a Western power to appease and therefore enthrone Islamic extremism and terror. After having been allowed to escape from house arrest in Paris, al-Husseini arrived in Cairo. He arrived one step ahead of Yugoslavia, which sought to indict him in absentia for crimes against humanity for his involvement in the genocide performed by the Hanzars against the Bosnian Serbs. In spite of his record, maybe possibly because of it, al-Husseini was granted full protection and royal treatment in Egypt and he was greeted upon his arrival by throngs who welcomed him as a hero.

In 1947, the Arab League, meeting in Aley, Lebanon, rejected the leadership of al-Husseini, who continued to insist on the total annihilation of Jewish Palestine, and favored that of the moderate Hashemite King Abdallah of Transjordan, who had hoped to absorb the Arab portions of Palestine west of the Jordan River into his kingdom and to forge a peace agreement with Jewish Palestine. By 1947, Jewish Palestine,

Amin al-Husseini at Arab League meeting at its cration—1944.

soon to achieve full sovereignty as Israel, was in the process of absorbing hundreds of thousands of European Jews who had had been rendered homeless and left in internment camps in postwar Europe.

King Abdallah of Transjordan was backed up in his moderate position by his nephew, Hassan II, the Hashemite king of Iraq, the Iraqi regent Emir Abd al-Ilah, Salih Jabr, the Iraqi prime minister, and other Arab leaders. Jabr was well aware of the destructive role al-Husseini had played in his instigating of the pro-Nazi coup in Iraq in 1941. The Arab League invaded Israel the moment the state was declared. Nevertheless, there was a real possibility in 1947 that some sort of a negotiation could have taken place between the Arab League and the Jews that could have led to a fair and equitable solution for both parties. The moderate King Abdallah, the brother of the Emir Faisal, maintained an open and cordial relation with representatives of the Yishuv.

After the Arab League snubbed al-Husseini in Aley, on the eve of the war with Israel, and after al-Husseini's cousin, Abd al-Qadir al-Husseini, was not appointed as commander of the Arab League forces according to al-Husseini's wishes, al-Husseini began to develop his own military force of irregulars, a militia that he called al-Jihad al-Muqaddas, or the Holy Warriors. Yasir Arafat started out as an arms supplier for the Holy Warriors and later, al-Husseini promoted Arafat and set him on the path toward literally inheriting his mantle, something that Arafat proceeded to do in every sense of the word. The Holy Warriors would engage in some of the fiercest fighting of 1948. There have been claims that Bosnian Hanzars and other former Muslim-Nazi fighters made their way into the ranks of the Holy Warriors, although there is no hard proof of this.

The intransigence of al-Husseini regarding his refusal to recognize Israel included his applying heavy pressure on Arab heads of state to reject U.N. Resolution 181 in 1947. U.N. Resolution 181, accepted by the Israelis but not by the Arabs under pressure from al-Husseini and at that point the Arab League, would have established a substantial Arab Palestinian state west of the Jordan River to exist alongside a severely truncated Jewish state consisting of little more than a few barely contiguous swaths of land along with the Negev desert.

Al-Husseini's fanaticism and intransigence was largely responsible for preventing the Palestinian Arabs, in 1947, from establishing a substantial Palestinian Arab state at peace with Israel. Instead, and too late in the game, as the war was raging, al-Husseini, who had previously been appointed as head of a reconstituted Arab Higher Committee, was also appointed as president of what was called the National Assembly, known as the All-Palestine Government, which, having been set up by the Arab Higher Committee Congress on October 1, 1948, briefly set up shop and attempted to govern a Palestinian Arab state within the confines of the Gaza strip.

The standard response from many Israelis and Jews when addressing the question of the Arab refugees who left Jewish Palestine in 1947–1948 is to recite the technically true but somewhat clichéd refrain that an approximate equivalent number of Jews living in the Arab world were also driven out of their homelands at the same time. The conventional Israeli and Jewish response to this issue is to accurately compare and contrast the incredibly effective job the nascent State of Israel did in terms of absorbing and integrating the newly arriving Jews in those years, people who were often poor and illiterate, to the miserable job the Arab states did regarding their treatment of their Arab brethren fleeing Palestine.

It is a well-known fact that a large number of Arabs who left Israel during this period, whether voluntarily or otherwise, were and remain forcibly confined to concentration-camp-like refugee camps and often live in bleak and wretched surroundings. The oil-rich Arab countries have prevented their fellow Arabs from assimilating into the population at large. It is also well known that the motivation for this obscene and inhumane behavior on the part of the Arabs toward their fellow citizens remains entirely political in nature. Al-Husseini played a key role in the early 1950s in discouraging the Arab states from absorbing the refugees. He often toured the camps and encouraged their leaders to be patient and await the liberation of Palestine and their return. These poor and misbegotten people serve as human pawns in a game plan to destroy Israel at a future date. The refugee camps also serve as spawning grounds for future terrorists.

Because of their generally high-minded values, many Israelis and Jews feel somewhat uncomfortable and squeamish over the issue of the Palestinian Arab refugees, which is why there is a tendency to deflect attention from the issue itself. At the core of the "right of return" for Arabs to Israel is the idea that those who left or who were driven out by Israel in 1947–1948 have a legitimate, and indeed, a superior claim over the Jews to sovereignty in Palestine. The principle they espouse, a principle that is almost universally accepted today by Arabs and Muslims and one that has even made substantial inroads in the Western democracies and even among certain segments of the Israeli and Jewish population, is that Israel is somehow occupying land that should be the home of another people and that these other people have a superior claim to sovereignty over the land.

The truth of the matter is that Israel has absolutely nothing to apologize for concerning the refugees who left in 1947–1948. Claims of the Palestinian Arabs to sovereign rights in Israel are entirely specious. When Haj Amin al-Husseini, the grand mufti of Jerusalem, returned to the Arab world after having collaborated with Hitler in Berlin during the war, a collaboration that directly involved the Holocaust, and after having enjoyed high and exalted status in Nazi Germany, he immediately resumed his effort to exterminate the Jews from Palestine. An entourage of Palestinian Arabs who had worked with him in Nazi Germany also joined him in his efforts. A network of pro-Nazi Arab groups, militias, and leaders supported him. Nazi money, which had been largely confiscated from the Jews of Europe, was also working its way into his grasp.

Furthermore, the reason there were refugees in the first place was because the Israelis did not kill or imprison the Arabs during the War of 1947–1948, but rather allowed them to flee. In fact, there is a substantial Arab minority within Israel today. This was in direct contrast to the al-Husseini-inspired Arab policy, which was to massacre any Jew unfortunate enough to fall behind their lines of advance. An example of this policy in action was when the Arab Legion sixth battalion captured the Jewish community of Kfar Etzion. The Jews surrendered and walked into the center of the town with their hands up. The Arab Legion "proceeded to mow them down," killing one hundred and twenty Jews. "Jews taken prisoner during convoy battles were generally put to death and often mutilated by their captors."[2]

In the two short years between the end of World War II, in May 1945, and the 1947 United Nations Resolution 181, which recognized a Palestine partitioned between a Jewish and an Arab sector, al-Husseini and his cohorts, working at breakneck speed, organized an Arab militia that would attempt to launch a genocidal assault against the Jews of Palestine in 1947. The Arab League launched a major military assault on all fronts on May 15, 1948. Even al-Husseini, in his memoirs written twenty years later, acknowledged the overwhelming superiority of the

Arab forces at the time. He explained away the Israeli victory, or the victory of what he referred to as "the aggressive Zionist entity," by making dark and ludicrous references to a British conspiracy:

> "Had a number of Arab groups not been deceived by promises made by the imperialists, and had they not operated on their own initiative and placed obstacles in the way of the Palestinian Arabs' Jihad . . . the Jews would not have established their aggressive entity in Palestine."[3]

It was in an atmosphere of genocide in every sense of the word that Israel began to rout out a population that was infiltrated with radicals who certainly opposed any national rights whatsoever for the Jews, and was likely honeycombed with cells that had every intention to carry out mass murder against Jews. There should be no doubt that a segment of the Palestinian Arabs, during this feverish period, and based upon the public utterances and actions of their leadership, posed a lethal threat to the very lives of every Jew in Palestine. Israel, under these conditions, had a moral right and a practical responsibility to act swiftly in an effort to remove the danger in order to protect the lives of its own people. At this critical time, al-Husseini was openly and unequivocally calling for a wholesale slaughter of the Jews of Israel, and given his involvement in the Nazi Holocaust, an involvement that was widely understood in Israel, there was absolutely no reason not to believe that he and his followers meant business.

Israel acted entirely within its right to self-defense, rights that are natural and that are recognized by international law and custom, in uprooting certain populations to the degree that they did this. Israel acted as any sane nation would and should act in a situation of like nature when it removed the threat to its people. An analogous theoretical situation would be if Al Qaeda cells, taking direction from Osama bin Laden, were operating in the U.S. and radicalizing segments of the Arab-American population. America would have a right, indeed a moral obligation, to remove the threat to its citizens and there would be no second-guessing such action. It should be stressed that while Israel's record was by no means pristine, that there were indeed a limited number of slaughters of innocent Arabs by Israel, nevertheless, under the circumstances of fighting a war for survival, a war that was both external as well as internal, Israel's record of minimizing the killing of innocent people is quite amazing and laudable. The overwhelming number of Arabs who left the country did so with a minimal amount of molestation. If the shoe were on the other foot, and al-Huesseini and the Arab League had emerged as the victors in 1947–1948, is there any doubt regarding the fate of the Jews?

David Ben-Gurion, who would be the first prime minister of Israel, had written that "It is the natural right of the Jewish people, like any other people, to control their own destiny in their sovereign state," and so, on May 14, 1948, Ben-Gurion declared Israel as an independent state and thus established unfettered sovereignty for the Jewish people in Palestine for the first time since the days of the Hasmonean Queen Salome over two thousand years previous.

The following day, May 15, the Arab League, in an attempt to kill Israel in the crib, invaded the infant state on all fronts with the combined force of seven Arab states. Participating in the slaughter of approximately 6,000 Jews, a mere three years after the defeat of Nazi Germany, were soldiers from Egypt, Jordan, Saudi Arabia, Syria, Lebanon, and Iraq, as well as irregulars from across the Arab world. There were reports that soldiers from the Nazi-Bosnian Muslim SS Hanzar divisions were seen on the front still wearing their distinctive Nazi uniforms. On May 15, 1947, Arab League Secretary General Abd al-Ahlman Azzam Pasha called for a jihad against the ancient Jewish state, declaring, "This will be a war of extermination and a momentous massacre which will be spoken of like the Mongolian massacres and the Crusades." al-Husseini concurred with Pasha when he said, "I declare a holy war, my Muslim brothers! Murder the Jews! Murder them all!"

By 1949, Israel had signed armistice agreements with all of the frontline Arab states. Soon after, substantial evidence suggests that al-Husseini arranged for the assassination of King Abdallah ibn-Hussein el Hashimi, the Hashemite king of Jordan. Abdallah was a significant rival to al-Husseini in his quest for power in Palestine, and Abdallah was on record as referring to al-Husseini, quite accurately I might add, as the very embodiment of the devil himself. King Abdallah was the brother of Emir Faisal, the hero of this book and the Arab leader who signed the Faisal-Weizmann Agreement. Abdallah shared many of Faisal's moderate tendencies and enlightened views. He expressed an interest in signing a formal peace agreement with Israel, but at the end of hostilities he failed to do so after buckling under the extreme pressures brought to bear by the Arab League. Al-Husseini was at least partially motivated in plotting the assassination of Abdallah, one of the many he would plot in his lifetime, by a desire for revenge over Abdallah's refusal to reappoint him as grand mufti of Jerusalem or to even let him visit Jerusalem.

King Abdallah of Jordan.

Abdallah's successors to the Jordanian throne, his son and grandson King Talal and King Hussein, also refused to reappoint al-Husseini as grand mufti. Both Talal and Hussein, acting out of a justifiable fear that al-Husseini would stir up trouble, banned him from entering either Jerusalem or Jordan. It should be noted that Jordan has since then proven to be a relatively moderate Arab state and very intolerant of Arab terrorism. At Abdallah's murder trial in Amman, it was revealed that al-Husseini had, according to testimony, been in contact with two of the conspirators to the assassination, both of whom would be convicted, in what was described as "the most dastardly crime Jordan ever witnessed." These two were Colonel Abdullah Tell, an ex-military governor of Jerusalem, and Dr. Musa Abdullah Husseini, who was Amin al-Husseini's cousin.

On July 16, 1951, the prime minister of Lebanon, Riad Bey al-Solh, was assassinated in Amman while visiting King Abdallah. Rumors were circulating at the time that al-Solh had come to Amman to discuss with Abdallah the possibility of signing a peace treaty with Israel. On July 20, 1951, four days after meeting alSolh and while in Jerusalem, King Abdallah himself would be assassinated while standing outside the al-Aqsa Mosque, where he was planning to deliver a eulogy for al-Solh. A Palestinian extremist who stated that he wanted to stop the king from making a separate peace with Israel, Mustapha Shukri Usho, fired three bullets into the king's head and chest. Abdallah's grandson, Hussein Ibn Talal, later King Hussein of Jordan from 1953 to 1999, was at the time standing at his grandfather's side. The young prince grappled with Usho until he was also shot. A medal pinned to the young Prince Hussein's chest at his grandfather's insistence had deflected the bullet and saved his life.[2]

In 1946, the Egyptian seventeen-year-old Mohammed Abder Rauf Arafat Al-Kudwa Al-Husseini, otherwise known by his nom de guerre Yasir Arafat, and who is said to be al-Husseini's nephew, met with al-Husseini in Cairo and began to work for him. Al-Husseini placed Arafat in charge of arms procurement for his fledgling irregular militia known as "The Holy Strugglers." al-Husseini was himself most likely the true founder of the al-Fatah party, which means "conquest" in Arabic. Fatah, Arafat's terror cell, would provide the nucleus of the PLO. Al-Husseini was probably responsible for arranging for Arafat, his protégé, to obtain the leadership position that set him on his way as one of the world's most preeminent terrorists. Arafat is on record as stating that he considers it to be an honor to walk in the footsteps of al-Husseini, and he has done just that in every respect.

With his record of violence against the Jews, his ruthlessness toward Arabs who seek peace with Israel, and his tight control over the considerable sums of money in PA coffers, Arafat has indeed continued to steadfastly forge ahead with the radical agenda of al-Husseini.

Arafat (far right) at al-Husseini eulogy (with mufti of Lebanon).

Al-Husseini had foolishly botched an opportunity to create a Palestinian Arab state in 1939 with the British White Paper and then again in 1947 with U.N. Resolution 181. Al-Husseini was blinded by his own extreme requirement of an all-Arab Palestine that would be as *judenrein*, or free of Jews, as the Europe envisioned by Hitler, even though al-Husseini would probably have a few token *dhimmi* Jews stick around in Palestine after he took over, those who could trace their ancestry back to the nineteenth century, to serve as sort of walking museum pieces. This Nazi-inspired idea was later formally codified into the Palestinian National Covenant. Al-Husseini's heir, Yasir Arafat, would also botch his opportunity to create another Palestinian Arab state in 2000 when he rejected the substantial concessions made by Israel at a meeting at Camp David in exchange for nothing more than an agreement to stop the genocidal program against the Jews of Israel. First al-Husseini and then Arafat would respond to the peaceful overtures from Israel by carrying out systematic and massive bloodbaths against innocent Jews.

In an August 2002 interview, Arafat called al-Husseini "our hero al-Husseini" because of his steadfast and uncompromising record of standing up to world pressure. Arafat was admiringly referring to the fact that al-Husseini had remained an Arab leader in spite of demands to have him replaced because of his Nazi ties. He compared al-Husseini's perseverance as comparable to his own rejection of pressure to reform the Palestinian Authority and to step aside.[3]

The PLO and today's Palestinian Authority retain the Nazi influence even though feeble attempts have been made to camouflage the Nazi trappings in the interest of preserving and furthering a burgeoning relationship with American and Israeli leftists. Ties between the PLO and various Nazi and pro-Nazi organizations are well documented and not denied. Joseph Farah, in his World Net Daily article "Roadmap to Nowhere," connects the terror cell Black September, responsible for the massacre of the Israeli athletes at the Munich Olympics, to Abu Mazen, the so-called "moderate" prime minister of the Palestinian Authority. The commander of the attack, Mohammed Daoud Oudeh, has stated that the Black September terrorists were working directly under the authority of al-Fatah and the authority of both Arafat and Abu Mazen. In 1995, when PLO cadets were preparing to take over the security of portions of Judea, Samaria, and Gaza, they were sworn into service with a straight-arm sig heil Nazi-style salute. Fawsi Salim el-Mahdi, who was the head of Arafat's praetorian guard known as Tanzim 17, which is now heavily involved in the intifada and possibly behind the suicide bombers, is better known to his associates by the nickname Abu Hitler, because he named his two sons Eichmann and Hitler.[4]

In 1962, Amin al-Husseini was appointed to lead the World Islamic Congress. This was his last public office and appearance. The congress drew up resolutions to cleanse the entire Arab world of its Jews, or to make the Arab world *judenrein*, or free of all Jews. Ancient and indigenous Jewish communities throughout the Arab world, communities that in many cases could trace their lineage back to centuries before the seventh-century Arab military conquest and occupation of the Middle East and North Africa, would find themselves under even more intense persecution and harassment than they had already been forced to endure.

The ethnic cleansing campaign against Middle Eastern and North African Jews, a campaign that was originally launched by al-Husseini in Palestine, would intensify in the 1970s; today, as a result, there are very few Jews left in the Arab world. Those Jews who remain live in a state of fear and exist in a state of informal detention. This last conference attended by al-Husseini would at long last mark the lowering of the curtain on his lengthy and loathsome public career, a career that was every bit as villainous and murderous as that of any one of the most vicious Nazi leaders. At the conclusion of the World Islamic Congress, al-Husseini mercifully and finally retired from public life to live out his remaining years in luxury in Beirut, where he would write his own very sanitized and politically expedient version of his life story. On July 5, 1974, in Beirut, Amin al-Husseini finally goose-stepped and sig heiled one last time as he marched and swaggered his way into his grave and what awaited him in the hereafter, completely unrepentant and utterly devoid of even a shred of conscience or compassion over the terrible suffering and death he had wrought on the world. Al-Husseini has left the world with a miserable and despicable legacy of hate and murder, a legacy that continues to thunder across the firmament of the Middle East.

Amin al-Husseini was one of those types of monsters who always maintained a quiet and cultured exterior. His ascetic face, neatly trimmed beard, penetrating blue eyes, and impeccable traditional Arab dress combined to affect a charismatic presence. Al-Husseini was also known to make a powerful and convincing argument. In a sense, he was like so many other utterly bloodless and immoral yet suave and sophisticated operators who stain the pages of human history. He could nonchalantly send a letter or utter a few sentences that could condemn tens of thousands to their deaths. In a sense, he was the classic archetype of the Nazi, or the Communist, or the totalitarian, in that he had absolutely no compassion, no humor, no scruples, no soul, and no humanity.

Postwar Nazis and Arab Terror

At the conclusion of World War II, al-Husseini would play a key role in what came to be known as Project Odessa, an operation that provided a pipeline for Nazi war criminals fleeing justice and making their way into Arab and Latin American countries. Francois Genoud, the arch-Nazi Swiss banker and private financier of al-Husseini, as well as other prominent and well-heeled former Nazis, would play a key role in the funding of this operation, primarily by using numbered Swiss bank accounts and drawing from monies that had largely originated from properties and capital that had been confiscated from Jewish victims as they were herded off to the death camps and crematoria. Genoud used these monies, derived from, among other forms of theft, the gold fillings of Jewish corpses, the gold having been extracted from the teeth of the Jewish corpse after the Jewish man or woman had been gassed in the death camps, to help postwar Nazis escape justice and also to fund the anti-Jewish and anti-Israel activities of al-Husseini and like-minded people and groups. The diabolical fact of the matter is that today's anti-Jewish and anti-Israel movement was largely established with monies that had been literally carved out of the hides of European Jews.

Thousands of Nazi war criminals would flee the advancing Allied forces and find safe havens in Egypt, Syria, and elsewhere in the post–World War II years. Al-Husseini maintained close contact with these Nazi expatriates in Cairo, a community that numbered in the several thousand, and also with Nazi expatriates in other Arab capitals and in other parts of the world. An example of al-Husseini-Nazi collaboration comes from American Nazi sympathizer H. Keith Thompson, who knew al-Husseini in those postwar years. Thompson reported, "I did a couple of jobs for him [al-Husseini], getting some documents from files that were otherwise unavailable." The fact is that informal postwar Nazi networks, spread out over several countries and continents, remained politically active, and that al-Husseini remained a key player in their ongoing plot against the Jews. Much of the financing of this network continued to flow from Swiss bank accounts filled with monies looted from Jews and very well may still.

Al-Husseini with Egyptian President Nasser.

The newly arriving Nazi war criminals would be quickly assimilated into Arab military, intelligence, and propaganda services. Many of these former Nazis had no problem converting to Islam, changing their names to Arab names, and assimilating into Arab society. Examples of this include an SS general who had commanded mobile Einsatzgruppen units in charge of murdering Ukrainian Jews and who would become a close friend and bodyguard for Egyptian President Gamel Abdel Nasser. Eichmann deputy Alois Brunner, convicted in absentia for war crimes at Nuremberg, would serve as an advisor to the Syrian general staff.[2] Otto Skorzeny, an SS officer described by the OSS as "the most dangerous man in Europe," and who led a rescue mission to free Mussolini from an Italian prison in 1943, would be employed by Nasser.

Other Nazis who made their way to Cairo after the war included Goebbels's aide Johannes von Leers, who converted to Islam and changed his name to Omar Amin. "If there is any hope to free the world from Jewish tyranny," von Leers-Amin wrote in a letter to American Nazi H. Keith Thompson, "it is with the Moslems, who stand steadfastly against Zionism, Colonialism and Imperialism." This same type of agitprop, with slight variations, emanates from the extreme left today. Von Leers, a.k.a. Omar Amin, became a top official in the Egyptian Information Ministry, which served as a haven for European Nazis and a major producer of anti-Jewish and anti-Israel propaganda that would creep across the Arab world. Nazi Louis Heiden, a.k.a. Louis al-Hadj, would translate Hitler's *Mein Kampf* into Arabic. *Mein Kampf* remains a perennial bestseller and blockbuster in much of the Arab world today. In his preface to *Mein Kampf*, al-Hadj states, "National Socialism did not die with the death of its herald. Rather, its seeds multiplied under each star."

The Egyptian government published and disseminated *The Protocols of the Elders of Zion*, the infamous Russian anti-Semitic forgery. *The Protocols* is accepted as gospel by the Nazis and is taken seriously today by extremists on both the far right and the far left. *The Protocols* is also widely disseminated in the Arab world today thanks to the influence of the Nazi expatriates and with help from the *Sonderfund*. In a nutshell, *The Protocols of the Elders of Zion* is an exposition of the classic conspiracy that cabals of elites are plotting to take over the world. The protocols themselves, listed in the book, are a sort of constitution for world government. The irony is that the so-called protocols in *The Protocols of the*

Elders of Zion are actually a close description of the Nazi and Communist programs, as opposed to anything even remotely related to any Jewish group or to Judaism. *The Protocols of the Elders of Zion* remains very much a part of the gospel of today's Islamic extremists and it is formally quoted in Article 32 of the charter of Hamas.

After the war and the death of his beloved Führer, Francois Genoud turned his attention and aspirations to the Arab world, which he viewed as the future vanguard for implementing the aims and goals of the defeated Third Reich. In the service of these goals, Genoud would involve himself in an airplane hijacking, he would underwrite attacks on Israel, and he would pay for the defense of Nazis and Jewish archenemies such as Adolf Eichmann, Klaus Barbie, and Carlos the Jackal. Besides using numbered Swiss bank accounts as clearinghouses in the trafficking of the confiscated money and property of European Jews, Genoud made a personal fortune publishing the posthumous writings of Hitler, Martin Bormann, and Joseph Goebbels. In the forward to *Hitler's Table Talk*, the diary of Martin Bormann, published by Genoud, the claim is made that Hitler, as part of his last will and testament, stated that he expected and hoped that the people of the Third World would carry on the work of the Thousand Year Reich.[3]

Genoud would become a major benefactor of Arab nationalism, as he would lavishly fund liberation movements in Morocco, Algeria, and Tunisia. Using the numbered Swiss bank accounts, Genoud transferred funds derived from Jewish victims to support various Arab causes. He set up and funded Arabo Afrika, an import-export company that served as a front for spreading anti-Jewish and anti-Israel propaganda in the Arab world and for delivering weapons to, among others, the Islamo-Marxist Algerian National Liberation Front (FLN). Many Nazis, including Hitler's bodyguard Major General Otto Ernst Remer, helped in shipping arms and providing military training for the FLN.

Genoud worked closely with the notorious former Reichbank director Hjalmar Schacht, who also remained a true believing Nazi after the war and who served as a conduit between the former Nazi infrastructure and the Arabs. Genoud and Schacht were certainly not the only Nazis who viewed the future of Nazism as residing in the Arab world. It is fascinating to note that neither Genoud nor Schacht, both major Nazi financiers and functionaries during the war, were ever substantially questioned by

Allied authorities or charged with a crime at Nuremberg, nor was either man ever convicted of any crime.[4]

In 1958, Genoud, along with Schacht, established the Arab Commercial Bank in Geneva to funnel funds to the Algerian separatists. At the time, the arch-Nazi central banker Schacht was quoted as having said, "National Socialism would conquer the world without having to wage another war." In 1962, after Algeria declared its independence from France, Genoud settled in Algiers and became the director of the newly created Arab Peoples' Bank, with Schacht lending assistance. After Genoud was arrested in Algiers for violating exchange control regulations in the transfer of $15 million of FLN money to a Swiss bank, Egyptian President Gamel Abdel Nasser interceded and Genoud was allowed to leave Algeria without having to stand trial. In November 1969, Genoud assisted left-wing lawyer Jacques Verges in his defense of three terrorists from the Popular Front for the Liberation of Palestine (PFLP) who were being tried for blowing up an El Al passenger plane in Zurich that February. Genoud arranged for all defense costs to be covered.[5]

Le Monde correspondent Jean-Claude Buhrer, who covered Francois Genoud for over three decades, reported that Genoud was directly involved in the February 21, 1972, hijacking of a Lufthansa Boeing 747, which, while preparing for takeoff in Bombay, India, and destined for Frankfurt, Germany, was seized by a group of Arab terrorists who conveyed to the Bombay control tower: "Call us the Victorious Jihad. If you call us Lufthansa, we won't answer you." Among the 181 passengers/hostages on board that day was nineteen-year-old Joseph Kennedy, the son of the late Senator Robert F. Kennedy.

The Palestinian terrorist Wadie Haddad coordinated the operation and Genoud assisted from Germany by carrying a ransom note to the Lufthansa offices in Cologne demanding $5 million in used bills for the "Organization for the Victims of the Zionist Occupation." The ransom note read as follows:

> A man carrying a suitcase with the money should wear a black jacket and gray pants, disembark at the Beirut airport holding *Newsweek* magazine in his left hand and the suitcase in his right hand, and go to the parking lot. With the key sent in the envelope from Cologne, he was to open an old Volkswagen parked under a sycamore tree and read the instructions on the rear seat.

Once the transaction was completed, the hijacked jet then flew to Yemen, where the passengers were released. The $5 million went to the Popular Front for the Liberation of Palestine (PFLP). This was the first operation of its kind, but certainly not the last. The $5 million would serve as seed money for future PFLP operations. Shortly before his suicide in 1998, Genoud admitted to his role in the hijacking, after presuming that the statute of limitations had run out, when he spoke of it to French biographer Pierre Pean. Genoud said, "The amount of money demanded of Lufthansa was very high . . . too low a number would have made us lose credibility. Too high a number might have made the operation fall through, especially considering how quickly the money had to be collected."

Genoud also revealed to Pean in the same interview that he had been working with the infamous master terrorist Carlos the Jackal since 1970. The murders of the Israeli athletes at the Munich Olympics occurred in 1972, the same year as the PFLP hijacking. Also involved in the Munich Olympics attack, according to Joseph Farah in his article "Roadmap to Nowhere," was Abu Mazen, who, as this book goes to press, is the prime minister of the Palestinian Authority. Farah reports, "The mastermind of the Munich Olympics massacre, Mohammed Daoud Oudeh, says it was Mazen who provided the money for the attack. Arafat and Mazen both kissed him on the cheeks before he set off to kill eleven Israeli athletes."[6] When one of the Black September murderers, Hassan Salameh, needed medical attention, Genoud quietly arranged for treatment at a private clinic in Lausanne.

Genoud would finance left-wing lawyer Jacques Verges in his defense of Gestapo chief Klaus Barbie, known as the Butcher of Lyon. In August 1987, the *International Herald Tribune* reported from Paris that "Francois Genoud, pro-Nazi Swiss banker living in Lausanne . . . who has been named several times in the French press as the trustee of the 'Nazi war chest,'" had been a backer of Wahid Gordji, an official in the Iranian embassy in Paris, who was implicated by a French court in various bombing attacks that killed thirteen persons in Paris in 1986. Those attacks were allegedly carried out by a pro-Iranian Islamic fundamentalist terrorist network.

Toronto author Erna Paris, in a book about Klaus Barbie, wrote that most of the money for these postwar Nazi-Muslim operations "was stolen from European Jews, and was deposited in numbered bank accounts through a clandestine club of former SS officers called Die Spinne (The Spider), the successor to the ODESSA organization."

Neo-Nazis have picked up the gauntlet from the Third Reich and have involved themselves in the Arab terror movement. One example out of many is the career of neo-Nazi Odfried Hepp who, after having bombed four U.S. Army bases in West Germany, fled to Tunis in 1982, where he joined the Palestine Liberation Front (PLF). One of West Germany's most wanted terrorists, Hepp was arrested in June 1985 while entering a PLF member's apartment in Paris. Four months later, PLF commandos seized the cruise ship *Achille Lauro* and murdered the elderly and wheelchair-bound American Jewish tourist Leon Klinghoffer. On the PLF's list of prisoners to be exchanged for the *Achille Lauro* hostages was none other than Odfried Hepp.

On November 8, 2002, Swiss police raided the home of a Swiss Nazi named Ahmad Huber as part of a dragnet involving an international banking group called Al Taqwa, which in translation means "Fear of God," which is linked to the Muslim Brotherhood. U.S. officials asked the Swiss to act on evidence they presented that indicated that Huber was a financial agent of Osama bin Laden. Evidence was seized from Huber's home indicating that he and the Al Taqwa group were acting as financial agents for several Muslim extremist groups including Hamas. Huber denied any involvement in terrorism and insisted that Al Taqwa was nothing more than a charity providing aid for needy Muslims.[7]

Germany's Office for the Protection of the Constitution described Huber as aspiring to be "a mediator between Islam and right-wing groups." In Huber's office are portraits of Hitler and SS chief Heinrich Himmler, along with photos of Islamic leaders and the French politician Jean-Marie Le Pen. In June 1994, Huber spoke at a mosque in Potomac, Maryland, about the "evils of the Jews." Journalist Richard Labeviere interviewed Huber about a meeting he attended in Chicago. Huber stated that the meeting brought together "the authentic Right and the fighters for Islam" and was where "major decisions were taken . . . the reunification is underway." Huber acknowledges that he attended meetings with Al Qaeda operatives in Beirut, Brussels, and London, and he's been quoted in the Swiss media as saying that Al Qaeda operatives "are very discreet, well-educated and highly intelligent people."

Neo-Nazis have lent support to al-Husseini protégé Saddam Hussein. Shortly before the 1991 Persian Gulf War, a group of German neo-

Nazis sought support from Saddam for the creation of an anti-Zionist legion of European neo-Nazi mercenaries. The neo-Nazi "Freedom Corps" arrived in Baghdad shortly before the 1991 Gulf War, where they were seen strutting around the streets in SS uniforms. Upon the commencement of hostilities, however, the Freedom Corps quickly packed their bags and scurried home.

Neo-Nazi Italian terrorist Stefano delle Chiaie, who is accused of masterminding a series of bomb attacks in Rome and Milan, wrote to Libyan dictator and likely al-Husseini protégé Colonel Muammar Gaddafi, urging him to form a united front against "atheistic Soviet Marxism and American capitalist materialism," both of which, delle Chiaie claims, are controlled by "international Zionism." With a few tweaks, this type of sloganeering could be mistaken for extreme leftist agitprop. Described in a 1982 CIA report as "the most prominent right-ist terrorist . . . still at large," delle Chiaie added in his letter to Gadaffi, "Libya can, if it wants, be the active focus, the center of national socialist renovation [that will] break the chains which enslave people and nations."

Colonel Gadaffi has from time to time supported neo-Nazi propaganda and terrorism. An Italian judicial inquiry found that the Libyan embassy in Rome aided in the escape of the Italian terrorist Mario Tuti shortly after a train bombing near Florence in 1974. Tuti was later captured and sentenced to a lengthy prison term for orchestrating the attack, which killed twelve and injured forty-four innocent people. The neo-Nazi National Front has disseminated *The Green Book*, Gadaffi's political manifesto in Britain. Former British Nazi leader Ray Hill reported that the Libyan People's Bureau financed an anti-Semitic supplement to the National Front's monthly magazine. Libya has financed junkets to Tripoli for neo-Nazis from England, France, Canada, the Netherlands, and several other countries.

The far-right-wing National Front, along with the black-supremacist Nation of Islam and also many left-wing groups, support the radical Islamist movement, and that support is mutual. Colonel Gadaffi, for example, gave Louis Farrakhan, head of the Nation of Islam, a $5 million interest-free loan in 1985. One year later, Farrakhan was officially welcomed in Libya, Saudi Arabia, and Pakistan. In Saudi Arabia, he was received by high officials in Jeddah and paid a courtesy call to the exiled Ugandan strongman Idi Amin. In Pakistan, he visited the Islamic fundamentalist Dictator General Zia-ul-Haq.

An unforeseen side effect of American support for the mujahideen free-dom fighters in their battle against the Soviet occupation of Afghanistan in the 1980s was the further development of radical Islamic terrorist cells, including Al Qaeda, and the development of a shadowy American black Muslim group called al-Fulqra. American Clement Rodney Hampton-El was one of several al-Fulqra volunteers in Afghanistan. Founded in 1980 by Pakistani Shiekh Mubarik Ali Jilani, the extremist Islamist al-Fuqra has been linked to seventeen murders and thirteen fire bombings in the U.S., mostly directed at rival Muslims. Hampton-El was convicted for his involvement in a bomb plot against the U.N. and other New York City landmarks in 1995 and was sentenced to thirty-five years in prison. Nine other terrorists were also convicted in that case, including Sheikh Omar Abdel Rahman, the blind Egyptian cleric who was already serving a life sentence for his role in the 1993 bombing of the World Trade Center, which resulted in six dead and over 1,000 injured. Hampton-El told an FBI informant that he had participated in a test explosion for the first attack on the World Trade Center.

The American Justice Department is presently investigating possible links between al-Fuqra and Osama bin Laden's Al Qaeda. Videotape has been found of a December 1993 meeting in the Sudan between al-Fuqra leader Shiekh Mubarik Ali Jilani and members of Islamic Jihad, Hamas, and, it is believed, Al Qaeda operatives. Federal officials also believe that al-Fuqra collaborated with Wadih el-Hage, who was sentenced to life in prison for conspiring with Osama bin Laden in the 1998 bomb-ings of the American embassies in Nairobi and Dar es Salaam.

In a manner not unlike the Communists and certain segments of the international left, neo-Nazis and the far right continue to make com-mon cause with the inheritors of the traditions set forth by Haj Amin al-Husseini, the grand mufti of Jerusalem. Since the September 11, 2001 attacks on America, both the far right and the far left have cham-pioned the radical Islamist cause. Also intertwined with both the far right and the far left is the Holocaust-denial industry, which is an example of rightists such as Mark Weber, David Irving, and Roberto Faurisson finding common cause with leftists such as Norman Finkelstein and Noam Chomsky. Needless to say, the works of this movement are treated as gospel in certain quarters of the Arab world.

Philosophically there is not much separating the views of al-Husseini and today's Nazis and Communists, as both political faiths embrace a

socialistic philosophy of government, which is to say a belief that government is an instrument of salvation that has a right to wield absolute power
over its citizens. Both political faiths also resonate with the idea of jihad,
called blitzkrieg by the neo-Nazis and "revolution" by the far left, as a
means of overpowering the non-believing world, especially the U.S.,
which all three groups view as the great Satan. Both Nazism and
Communism have a long and sordid history of intertwining and interlock-
ing interests and cooperation. Many infamous examples can be cited where
any combination of these two political faiths have formed, to use a term
coined by the notorious Communist propagandist of the 1930s Willi
Münzenberg, a "united front." The free world, and freedom itself, remains
the obstacle standing in the path of these bloody anti-human utopians.

*Militants of the Palestinian ruling Fatah party salute
during a pre-election rally for the students council at the
Al-Quds University in the West Bank town of Hebron—
Monday March 21, 2005.*

Postwar Communists and Arab Terror

The grand mufti of Jerusalem was at the forefront of the movement that gave birth to the modern imperialistic strain of Islam, a strain
that predominates today in much of the Arab and Islamic world. The
ways of al-Husseini would largely sweep aside and supplant the more
progressive ways of the Emir Faisal ibn Hussein, who represented a
progressive movement toward the development of strong and sovereign
Arab and Islamic states based on democratic institutions and principles.
Faisal believed that the Arab states would grow and develop as a result
of maintaining a peaceful and productive relationship with Israel and
the Western democracies.

In the 1930s, Hitler and his peculiar brand of authoritarian socialism
would come to dominate the so-called Arab street, with al-Husseini as
its most influential proponent. Nazism appealed to the more regressive
strain existing in Islam in the same way that both Nazism and left-wing
Communism appealed to the more regressive strain existing in Europe.
The relationship between the two authoritarian faiths, that of Hitler
and that of al-Husseini, would reach a zenith of influence during World
War II when the two leaders literally became partners in a conspiracy to
dominate the world, destroy the Western democracies, and annihilate

the Jewish people. After the defeat of Hitler in 1945, Nazism and Nazi networks continued to maintain considerable and deadly influence in Arab and Islamic countries. After the war, al-Husseini continued to play a key role in furthering the goals and ideas of postwar Nazism, as illustrated in the last chapter.

There is, however, no question that in the period following World War II and to the present day, the Communist movement, as embodied by the Soviet Union, which had emerged victorious after the war, and the Soviet satellites and international communism in general, would largely supplant Nazism as the primary sponsor of al-Husseini-inspired imperialistic Islamic terrorism. Today, the international left remains a tacit fifth column for Islamic terror in the West by making common cause with the Islamic terrorist infrastructure. The nature of that convergence of interests is the shared values of an anti-democratic, anti-Western, anti-Israel, and anti-American agenda.

By the early 1950s, Hassan al-Banna, the founder of the secret society known as the Muslim Brotherhood, had begun to openly identify himself with and promulgate the ideas and tactics of communism, ideas that he began to introduce into the Islamic fundamentalist movement. During this period, much of the revolutionary jargon, style of agitation, propaganda, and victimology mythology in the Arab world began to take on a distinctly leftist coloration, not that this was all that much of a departure from the previous Nazi-style jargon, which was demonstrably of a like nature. A young Yasir Arafat, a likely nephew and protégé of al-Husseini, was active in the Muslim Brotherhood in those years.

In 1956, Arafat and two of his comrades, Salah Khalaf and Khalil al-Wazir, all leaders of a militant student group loosely affiliated with the Muslim Brotherhood, were invited to participate in the "Prague World Festival of Youth," which was a training seminar for young Communists and potential recruits into the international Communist apparatus. After attending the "festival," Arafat and his two cohorts, using forged passports, went on to Stuttgart, West Germany, which was at the time known to have a large population of Marxist Palestinian Arabs. Khalef and al-Wazir, along with Palestinian Arab activist Khalid Hasan, stayed on in Stuttgart, where they facilitated, with Soviet backing, the development of secretive Communist-Muslim terror cells. These left-wing Arab cells, often intertwining their activities with their close Nazi soul mates Francois Genoud, Hjalmar Schacht et al., would assist in supporting the Islamo-Marxist Algerian NLF in the early 1960s.

Around this time, Arafat set up the terrorist cell known as al-Fatah, which would later form the controlling center of the umbrella of terrorist groups known as the Palestine Liberation Organization (PLO). Al-Fatah would further solidify its alliance with the Communist Soviet Union after the 1967 Six-Day War against Israel and again after the 1973 Yom Kippur War and the subsequent expulsion of Soviet advisors from Egypt. Starting in 1974, approximately 1,000 PLO operatives would be sent each year to the Soviet Union or to one of the Eastern European satellites, where they would be trained in military and terror tactics by KGB experts or by their Eastern European counterparts.

In the 1980s, most of the advanced training of the PLO terrorists was conducted at a special Soviet military academy for foreigners in Simferopol, a Crimean port on the Black Sea. Recruits would undergo a strict six-month course, which included basic military field maneuvers, communications, lectures in military theory, the "engineering" of terrorism, as well as a basic background in Marxism. PLO observer to the U.N. Zehdi Terzi confirmed that "the Soviet Union and all the socialist countries . . . open their military academies to some of our freedom fighters . . . . There is no secret that our boys go to the Soviet Union; they go to the socialist countries for their training. We are getting our machine-guns, RVJ's, and explosives" from the Soviets.

International terrorism expert Yossef Bodansky, in his book *Target America*, writes on Soviet coordination with Islamic terrorists. Bodansky writes of the 1972 Baddawi Conference held at the Baddawi refugee camp in Lebanon and co-chaired by Marxist terror leader George Habash. Yevgeny Primakov, the head of the Soviet KGB and fluent in Arabic, also co-chaired the conference. The conference established a worldwide "alliance of progressive movements and terrorist organizations," which would include, besides the PLO umbrella, terrorist cells from Europe and the Third World. From this point on, international terror would receive a large measure of funding, coordination, and propaganda support directly from the Kremlin, and this support would find resonance in the vast network of left-wing media, academic, and intellectual echo chambers that are found in every corner of the globe. Propaganda and agitation support continues to this day, long after the collapse of the evil empire.

The central Communist theory at play at the Baddawi Conference was that acts of terror, the murder of innocent people, and the mayhem that would result would undermine the Western democracies and would eventually lead to a socialist victory. According to the TV documentary *The Russian Connection*, which consisted of a series of interviews with several members of the PLO, no terrorist attack against Israel would occur without Soviet consultation. The PLO itself boasted at the time of Arafat's weekly meetings in Beirut with Soviet ambassador and KGB officer Alexander Soldatov. According to the documentary, the Soviets lent support to the PLO in the form of arms, training, planning, and propaganda.

The strategy emerging from the Baddawi Conference is a classic example of the Marxist dialectic in action. In the 1970s, the international Communist movement understood that the Western democracies, with their traditions of freedom, private property, individual rights, and Judeo-Christian beliefs, would never willingly succumb to international socialist control either willingly or without a fight. The theory that held sway at the conference was that terror would succeed where a military assault would fail in terms of weakening the resolve of these societies to survive. Besides, terror was cheaper and easier than war.

The decisions made at Baddawi were derived from the thinking of Communist theoreticians of the past such as Italian Communist Antonio Gramsci who, in his famous prison diary, wrote of the "long march through the institutions" as a means of subduing the West. Like the Baddawi theoreticians, Gramsci understood that the West would not buckle under an external assault, but would have to be softened up and imploded from within. This uniquely Communist approach and contribution to the philosophy of world domination is quite different and stands apart from the more conventional Nazi blitzkrieg or Islamist jihad.

The first coordinated terror attack after Baddawi, an attack that was as a direct result of the Baddawi agenda, occurred on April 11, 1974, when terrorists hijacked a bus in Quirat Shemona, Israel, and murdered eighteen innocent people, including eight children, on the bus. On the heels of this "action," May 15, 1974, terrorists crossed into Israel from Lebanon and seized a nursery school in Maalot, Israel. The terrorists sprayed the infants and children with machine gun fire and grenades as they crouched on the floor, killing twenty-eight and injuring dozens.

In an article in *The Wall Street Journal* (Sept. 22, 2003) entitled "The

KGB's Man," former Romanian Communist chief of intelligence Ion Mihai Pacepa reports that before defecting to the U.S. from Romania, he was responsible for giving Yasir Arafat about $200,000 per month in laundered money throughout the 1970s. He also reports that he sent two cargo planes stuffed with uniforms and supplies to Beirut each week during this period. When Pacepa first met Arafat, he bragged that he had invented the hijackings of airplanes. In 1972, according to Pacepa, Arafat was placed on the intelligence services' top priority list in the Soviet Union and many Eastern Bloc satellites.

The international left has generally thrown its lot in with the Islamists, and many are fully witting regarding the possible conse-quences to Western civilization. Besides supporting the failed "Zionism Is Racism" resolution at the United Nations Conference on Racism in Durban, South Africa, in September 2001, which was sponsored by the Islamists who had intensively prepared for this vote for over a year and who lavished funds on their supporters, leftists have generally made common cause with the Islamists by embracing anti-Zionist propa-ganda. While much of the radical left supports and even collaborates with the terrorists outright, much of the world's establishment leftist elite continues to ally itself with the genocidal program against Israel by applying pressure on Israel to make dangerous concessions to the Palestinian Arab leadership.

In all fairness, most leftists are unwitting participants in a policy of appeasement and surrender. Their approach is strikingly similar to the one that had been employed by the liberal British Prime Minister Neville Chamberlain in the 1930s, in his quest for peace with Hitler. As he waved that white paper and proclaimed "peace in our time" to that soggy crowd standing in the rain to greet him upon his return from meeting with Hitler in Munich, a paper that allowed Hitler to scarf down large slices of Czechoslovakia, Neville Chamberlain, a well-meaning liberal, was also unwitting to the true nature of the enemy he was dealing with.

Classic left-wing propaganda has been routinely employed against the State of Israel, particularly since the Israeli War in Lebanon in the early 1980s. In classic agitprop style, those who seek to delegitimize and destroy Israel will invariably try to portray the conflict as one between a mammoth military power, Israel, and an aggrieved victim, the vast and oil-rich Arab and Islamic world. The left likes to particularly emphasize the fact that Israel receives considerable military aid from the U.S. Many on the left concur with elements of the radical Islamists in the view that the U.S. is the great Satan. America has always been the number one obstacle to the creation of a utopian world socialism in the minds of many leftists. The fact that Israel has legitimate and obvious security needs is downplayed and even scoffed at.

The fact is that Israel, acting as any sane sovereign state would in like circumstances, has developed a strong and able military. This ought to be and certainly is a great source of pride. Is there any doubt that if this were not the case, Israel would have been annihilated long ago? The reality of the situation becomes more obvious when one engages in a conversation with those who complain about Israeli military strength. Israel has a moral and practical right and an obligation to its citizens to maintain as strong a military position as possible, especially under the circumstances.

The Palestinian Arab leadership and elite have successfully employed the left-wing tactic of victimization to whip up support for their own cause and violence against Israel and Israeli Jews. Israel is characterized as the oppressor and the Israeli military and individual Israelis are portrayed as cruel and atrocious. The fact that the Palestinian Arab leadership is to blame for scotching many opportunities for sovereignty west of the Jordan, which would have occurred alongside a sovereign Israel, a policy that stretches back to al-Husseini's rejection of the Peel Commission in 1934, is either ignored or openly embraced as justified by the "occupation," which, in this view, constitutes any Jewish sovereignty in Palestine. Regarding the atrocity propaganda employed against the Israeli military and Israelis in general, this is nothing more than a variation of the old blood libel, a vicious medieval Christian lie that claimed that Jews killed gentile babies to use their blood to bake Passover matzo.

Denouement

Amin al-Husseini organized a gang of thugs and launched a reign of terror in Palestine by killing innocent Jews praying at the Wailing Wall in Jerusalem. The terror against the Jews, as well as against moderate Arabs, has been raging ever since. Shortly after al-Husseini instigated the 1920 slaughter, the British Mandatory authorities appointed him as grand mufti of Jerusalem and subsequently to other political positions, thus bestowing upon him the power of leadership over Palestinian Arabs. This would be the first of many subsequent appeasements by the Western powers to Arab and Islamic terrorism. This policy has allowed Islamic terror to thrive in the world. Britain tried to appease the Nazis in 1938 when British Prime Minister Neville Chamberlain acquiesced to the divvying up of Czechoslovakia. While Hitler and his Nazi terrorists were eventually defeated, the Islamic terrorist disciples of al-Husseini remain at large. Al-Husseini launched terror against Jews in Palestine in 1921, 1929, and in the Nazi-backed 1936-1939 Arab Revolt. As the British-appointed leader of the Palestinian Arabs, al-Husseini drove out and assassinated moderate Arab leaders who opposed his radical agenda, a process that continues unabated.

In 1937, after meeting with the Nazi official Adolf Eichmann in

Palestine, a meeting that was quickly followed by al-Husseini's deportation from Palestine by the British, he began a close association with the Third Reich and began to use his influence in the Arab world, an influence that had been considerably enhanced over the years, to move the Arabs into the Nazi orbit of Hitler, his sponsor. He would replicate his career in Palestine throughout the Arab world by assisting in the establishment of Nazi-Muslim organizations in Arab capitals, which would harass Arab moderates in their respective countries as al-Husseini himself had done in Palestine.

Much of the ruling Arab elite would later emanate from these organizations, including such al-Husseini protégés as Gamel Abdel Nasser, Saddam Hussein, Yasir Arafat, Osama bin Laden, and countless others. As a paid Nazi agent, al-Husseini promoted collaboration with the Third Reich and played a major role in instigating the failed pro-Nazi Golden Square coup in Iraq in 1941. After declaring a jihad against the British after the failure of the Iraqi coup, al-Husseini fled to Nazi Germany, where he established his headquarters for the duration of the war.

While in Nazi Germany, al-Husseini was installed as the de facto head of a Muslim-Nazi government-in-exile. His mission in Germany was essentially to promote the Holocaust against the Jews of Europe and to promote Nazism in the Arab world. Hitler personally promised him that he would be the führer of the Arab world and that he would head a new Nazi-Muslim social order after the Nazis emerged victorious in Europe and militarily crossed the Caucasus. Al-Husseini's support of Hitler was also predicated on the promise that after Hitler liquidated European Jewry, he would assist in a Holocaust against the Jews of Palestine and of the entire Arab world (*Appendix D*).

Al-Husseini's unique brand of Nazism, a merge between modern scientific socialistic Nazism and a strain of fundamentalist Islam, would make profound inroads into the Arab world during the war, an influence that continues to metastasize today, as evidenced by the continuing genocidal program against the Jews of Israel. The Nazis did not by any means confine themselves to killing Jews, and likewise the radical Islamic terrorists do not, as witnessed on September 11, 2001. The difference between Hitler's Nazism and that of al-Husseini and his Nazi-Muslims should ultimately be viewed as strictly cosmetic in nature.

While in Nazi Germany, al-Husseini helped to form and train Muslim-Nazi SS Hanzar brigades that would directly participate in a program of genocide against Christian Serbs, Jews, and Roma in the Balkans. The influence and legacy of the Hanzars is manifesting itself today in Muslim Bosnia, Kosovo, Albania, and parts of Macedonia. Al-Husseini, it should be noted, began his career as an officer in the Turkish Army during World War I, at a time when Turkey was conducting genocide against their indigenous Armenian and Greek Christian populations. Al-Husseini always spoke admiringly about Ottoman imperialism.

Al-Husseini was directly and intimately involved in the Holocaust against the Jews of Europe. His many broadcasts and letters to Nazi and pro-Nazi leaders attest to this. He was a firsthand witness to the death camps, as photos attest. Before the war, during the war operating from Berlin, and up until the time of his death, al-Husseini helped funnel Nazi money, largely money confiscated from Jews, into the Arab world in order to promote anti-Jewish and anti-Israel propaganda, sabotage, and terror. Al-Husseini was directly and decisively involved in the Nazi attempt to annihilate the Jewish people and he would transfer that involvement into the Arab world, thus directly contributing to an ongoing program of genocide against the Jews of Israel and the Arab world.

Perhaps the penultimate modern practitioner and believer in what has been called muftism, the philosophy of Amin al-Husseini, would be Osama bin Laden. Like al-Husseini, bin Laden believes in the divine rule of sharia over the Islamic world or the Dar es-Salaam. This means, in practical terms, no individual freedom, no democracy, and severe punishment for those who refuse to submit to a set of arbitrary laws, rules, and statutes imposed by a dictator claiming to derive authority from Allah.

In an interview published in the Arabic newspaper *al-Quds al-Arabi* and republished in London on February 23, 1998, bin Laden proclaimed a jihad in the name of the "World Islamic Front." This term "World Islamic Front" offers an interesting intermingling between the traditional obligation of the Muslim to engage in jihad against the Dar al-Harb, or the World of War, that being the portion of the world that has yet to submit to Islam, and a modern revolutionary left-wing posturing regarding the formation of a "front" or a vanguard.

By jihad, bin Laden did not mean the more moderate and modern extrapolation of the term, the one that is popular with more moderate Muslims in America, the one which connotes an internal struggle against evil, but by jihad, bin Laden meant the literal and classic meaning of the term, which is a call for a bloody holy war. In the *al-Quds al-Arabi* interview, bin Laden implored devout Muslims "to kill Americans and their allies, both civil and military . . . . By God's leave, we call on every Muslim who believes in God and hopes for reward to obey God's command to kill the Americans and plunder their possessions wherever he finds them and whenever he can. Likewise we call on the Muslim ulema and leaders and youth and soldiers to launch attacks against the armies of the American devils and against those who are allied with them from among the helpers of Satan . . . for those who respond to this call, the conflict is clearly a war to the death between Muslims and unbelievers, the latest phase in a struggle that has been going on for more than fourteen centuries since the time of the Prophet Mohammed, the revelation of the Koran, and the advent of Islam."

Throughout his life, al-Husseini called for jihad against the infidel, which in his day meant the Zionist Jew and the British. Additionally, al-Husseini called for jihad against those he determined to be Muslim apostates, or those Muslims who engaged in virtually any relations with the Zionists or the British. Al-Husseini was a driving force behind much of the terror and many of the assassinations against Muslims that occurred in his lifetime and, subsequently, he bears a large responsibility for the destruction of any moderate and modernizing Muslim movement. Conversely, al-Husseini proved to be a driving force behind the regressive phenomenon of Islamic terrorism.

Al-Husseini tapped into and modernized an ancient and imperialistic precept of Islam, a precept that demands the total submission of those living within its sphere of influence while at the same time calling for a perpetual jihad against those living in the portion of the world that refuses to submit. In this sense, among others, the beliefs of al-Husseini and his followers resonate with that of the modern socialism of German Nazism. Like radical Islam, Nazism demanded a high level of conformity from its citizens (Sharia) and sought to establish a new social order through expansion and conquest (jihad). Radical Islamists follow passages in the Koran and other Islamic texts that clearly and unequivocally call for the slaughter of those who are perceived as standing in the way of the Islamic utopia, which is similar to the Nazi justification for the Holocaust. Nazism provided both the physical and spiritual bridge by which modern Islamic extremism could establish a beachhead.

It should be viewed as no coincidence that after the collapse of Nazism in 1945, left-wing communism would step in and fill the power vacuum by aligning itself with radical Islam. It was this left-wing Islamist axis that was successful in spearheading the effort to get Zionism declared as racism at the United Nations Conference on Racism held in Durban, South Africa, in September 2001. This effort had been a year in the making and was viewed as a major step by its sponsors toward delegitimizing the State of Israel. One of those glaring coincidences of history occurred three days after U.S. Secretary of State Colin Powell courageously walked out of that conference. Three days after America took a moral stand against the leftist-Islamist agenda, hijacked planes destroyed the World Trade Center in New York City.

Like its philosophical soul mate Nazism, as well as is the case with radical Islam, modern communism has also sought to totally control its citizens (sharia) and has sought to expand its realm through conquest (jihad, blitzkrieg). Like today's radical Islamists who are attempting to conduct a holocaust against those who refuse to submit, and like the Nazis who in fact did conduct a Holocaust against those who they deemed as racially impure, the Communists conducted what author R.J. Rummel referred to as "Democide," which is the mass murder of those living within their realm, whom they viewed as not politically correct or as standing in the way of their socialist progress (sharia). In their great and glorious march toward their sunlit socialist future, the Communists liquidated over 100 million people in the twentieth century (jihad) according to the well documented *Black Book of Communism*.

Learning from his collaborator, Hitler, al-Husseini introduced into the Arab world the hysterical and bizarre belief that utopia and salvation is obtainable on earth if and when the Jewish people are sacrificed on the altar. While these ideas are to a degree embedded into a virulent strain of Islam going back to the founding of the faith, nevertheless, Nazism lent a modern scientific veneer to certain old Islamic ideas in a manner that is not unlike the role modern left-wing communism has had in resurrecting and updating the old and authoritarian oriental concept of the divine right of kings. It should be noted that Europe endured two colossal and bloody world wars and a cold war before such ancient and authoritarian ideas were placed into remission.

A core belief in the Arab world today, a world that remains gripped by the old and earthly notions of authoritarianism, notions that are enhanced by international, primarily left-wing fifth columnists, holds that if Israel and the Jewish people are eliminated, or at least if they are turned into slaves, somehow everything will suddenly turn bright and rosy. This intensely held belief has even been embraced by its adherents as a personal manifesto, as many individual Arabs, like their Nazi predecessors, have actually stooped to blaming Israel and Jews for every problem in the universe, including even their own personal misfortunes. This hateful embrace has led to a twisted phenomenon of a culture that thinks, for example, that it's a big mitzvah to blow up innocent Jewish men, women, and children to smithereens with suicide bombers.

Let me reiterate at this point that muftism, the legacy of Haj Amin al-Husseini, was not, is not, and will never be an inevitability in the Arab and Islamic world. Arab peoples today should be encouraged to support enlightened Muslim leaders, those who walk in the footsteps of the Emir Faisal, such as Sheikh Abdul Hadi Palazzi. Such a path will lead to a true fulfillment of the most positive aspects of the Islamic dream. Medieval European imperialism, Japanese imperialism, communism, and Nazism all represented imperial and oppressive movements in their day, all of these movements sought submission from their own citizens and plunder from their neighbors, and all of these movements attracted the support of destructive and amoral radicals.

Some of these world order faiths were defeated on the battlefield while others withered away gradually over centuries. As this book goes to press, America has, under the wise leadership of President George W. Bush and his counselors, rediscovered its moral compass and is responding vigorously and decisively against the terror attack of September 11, 2001. Out of both moral conviction and out of practical national security concerns, America has now defeated the radical Islamist regimes of Afghanistan and Iraq. Whether these positive developments set in motion a trend toward peace and enlightened freedom in the Islamic world, as envisioned by the Emir Faisal, remains at this point an open question.

Muftism grew and, with Nazi backing, matured and blossomed into what is today a malevolent and cancerous communistic Islamo-Fascist movement. The practical cost of muftism for the Arab and Islamic world has been millions of people living in wretched poverty and squalor with few rights and few freedoms. The one-party Islamic dictatorships and kingdoms stifle opposition and these regimes remain in ascendance with no end in sight at this point. Violence and atrocities against women and religious minorities, slavery, and genocidal programs remain a part of daily life in certain sections of the Islamic world. There is little if any respect for individual human life in these putrid and stultifying societies.

The spiritual cost of muftism to the Arab and Islamic world is the spectacle of generations of Arabs infused with and contorted by an unquenchable hatred for the non-Muslim world in general and for America and Israel in particular. International leftist victimization propaganda continues to play into the hands of the Arab ruling classes, who shift the blame for their own failed and torpid societies and economies on to the backs of the blameless nations of the free world. Meanwhile, right under the very soils and sands of many of these Arab nations are some of the world's largest oil reserves.

The Western democracies are now reaping the bloody harvest for having ignored and even appeased this spiritual disease of muftism, a virulent form of a cancer of the soul that is now metastasizing. The harvest of our obsolescence, along with our seeming unwillingness to assert our natural and moral prerogative to defend the lives and properties of our people and the future of our sovereign and free nations, has been an increasing campaign of cold-blooded murder of innocent men, women, and children. It should be clear that the radical Islamists view peace gestures from the Western powers as acts of defeat and surrender. Americans are beginning to show signs of recognizing the true nature of the political and spiritual disease that is presently afflicting much of the world and continues to spread, and are taking proactive actions to stanch the flow of blood and oppression.

Today, America is, at long last, starting to stand up for itself and the free world, not to mention for the long-suffering and oppressed Muslim peoples, as America begins to shoulder a major share of the moral and material opposition to this evil force. In the process, America is reawakening to the true meaning of its creed as Americans, particularly since the dastardly events of September 11, and are recognizing that freedom and liberty do not grow on trees, but rather that these rights, while given by the creator and natural to man, nevertheless have to be earned and defended from time to time if necessary. America is also reawakening to the fact that there really is such a thing as an identifiable good and evil in the universe. Decades of moral relativity and the counter-culture stand to implode on their own contradictions.

Only time will tell in terms of which legacy, that of Emir Faisal ibn Hussein or that of Haj Amin al-Husseini, the grand mufti of Jerusalem, will ultimately emerge as the guiding model for the Islamic world. Ultimately, and inevitably, freedom will prevail and progress will be restored. The only question of relevance, the only question that must be confronted by freedom-loving peoples everywhere, is at what cost freedom? How much murder, violence, social anarchy, poverty, dissolution, and hate will have to transpire before freedom is re-asserted?

Given the potential of accessibility of today's weapons of mass destruction to terrorists, and given the increased and even likely possibility that those weapons could fall into the hands of some of these fanatical evildoers, there is little time to spare. The free world no longer has the luxury or even the option of indulging itself in denial. The cost of such a denial is too frightful to contemplate at this juncture of history. We have all been made well aware of the frightful cost of denial, a cost that has already been paid in rivers of innocent blood.

The perfect metaphor for the nature of the conflict we are now embroiled in, a metaphor that we must never forget, is that awful day when nineteen radical Islamists, acting in concert with an international network of terror with the encouragement and support of several Arab and Islamic regimes, hijacked those private American passenger planes, planes filled with innocent people, and used those planes to blow up and destroy the World Trade Center and the Pentagon on September 11, 2001. We must never forget that deadly date, a date in which over three thousand of our fellow free and peace-loving citizens were cruelly and callously murdered for having had the audacity to not submit to Dar el-Islam. That date of infamy was the day that the frontier of the grand mufti and his Nazi partner Adolf Hitler finally but inexorably moved right into the very heart of the United States of America.

AMERICA WILL NEVER FORGET SEPTEMBER 11, 2001.

Rapprochement

The enlightened example of Emir Faisal ibn Hussein and of like-minded Muslims stood in direct contrast to that of al-Husseini, both politically and spiritually. Emir Faisal envisioned a future in which fully sovereign, prosperous, and independent Arab and Islamic states would coexist peacefully with their non-Muslim neighbors and with each other. His hope for the Arab and Islamic states was that they would develop over time into full democracies with freedom and liberty and in complete control over their respective destinies. Emir Faisal, a traditional as well as a modern Muslim leader, and a nationalist in the best meaning of the term, represented the more positive aspects of Islamic faith and culture, the aspects that most Westernized Muslims in this country talk about and claim to support. Emir Faisal wanted the Arab and Islamic states to live in peace with their non-Muslim neighbors and thus to emerge as free and prosperous states interacting with the civilized world.

A modern example of an enlightened Arab leader, cut from the same cloth as Emir Faisal is Sheikh Abdul Hadi Palazzi, the secretary general of the Italian Moslem Association. Sheikh Palazzi cites traditional Islamic texts when he supports Jerusalem as the undivided capital of a Jewish state. While speaking at Congregation Shomrei Emunah on March 7,

2003, Sheikh Palazzi stated, "The idea that Islam should prevent Arabs from recognizing any sovereign right of Jews over Palestine is quite recent and can by no means be found in Islamic classical sources . . . All parties must understand that Jews should never agree to have fewer rights than the other religions, and Israelis will never agree to see David's capital divided into two parts." Palazzi also explained to the congregants that Mecca is sacred to Islam and Rome is sacred to Catholicism in the same way as Jerusalem is sacred to Judaism.[1]

Sheikh Palazzi, who received his Ph.D. in Islamic studies from Sheikh Abdul Aziz Ibn Baz, the grand mufti of Saudi Arabia and a leader of the Jerusalem-based Root & Branch Association, explained to the congregants that both the Torah and the Koran unequivocally support the notion that G-d, communicating through his servant Moses at Sinai, liberated the children of Israel (Jacob) from bondage in Egypt in order to establish them in the Promised Land. Palazzi pointed out that the Koran, in Sura 17:104, explicitly calls for a reassertion of sovereignty for the Jews in the land of Israel before the last judgment:

> And, thereafter, We [Allah] said to the children of Israel: 'Dwell securely in the Promised Land. And when the last warning will come to pass, We [Allah] will gather you [the children of Israel] together [in Israel] in a mingled crowd.

Sheikh Palazzi has stated that the holiness of Jerusalem to Islam is derived from the teaching that the Prophet Mohammed ascended to heaven on a flying steed from the Holy Rock, which is located inside the Dome of the Rock on the Temple Mount. This spiritual event, Palazzi asserts, has no relation to Jewish sovereignty in Jerusalem, since at the time of the Prophet's accent, Jerusalem was under the control of the Byzantine Empire and not the Jews. Sheikh Palazzi takes issue with what is apparently an official line of the Palestinian Authority concerning Jewish claims in Jerusalem, which is that Solomon's Temple never even existed at the Temple Mount. In refuting this claim, a claim that is also refuted by archeological evidence, Sheikh Palazzi cites the Koran, which instructs the Muslim to face Mecca in prayer (*qibla*) and the Jew to pray (*qibla*) facing the Temple that one stood in Jerusalem. Palazzi notes that the Koran quotes the Prophet as stating that he had no problem inviting Jews to pray alongside him, according to their tradition.

Sheikh Palazzi vigorously refutes the Muslim extremist position that Islam is at war with Judaism. This was the position embraced by al-Husseini and remains a mainstay of the Muslim Brotherhood, the Wahabi sect, Hamas, and extremist Islamic groups in general. Palazzi insists that a Hadith, cited by the terrorists, that they claim calls for the killing of Jews is misinterpreted. Palazzi states: "There is no indication that Muslims are supposed to kill Jews before the end of days. Most classical scholars consider the verse to be a prophesy of something that was to happen after the verse was written. It might refer to a war that was coming or perhaps it referred to this terrible conflict we see now. But before Hamas, no Muslim scholar ever interpreted the verse to mean that there was going to be a global war between Jews and Muslims."

Sheikh Palazzi, echoing Emir Faisal, stated, on the occasion of a bus bombing in Haifa that killed fifteen people and injured dozens, that "the world and civilized nations" should consider the Palestinian Authority as "a gang for promoting terror, educating children in terror from elementary school age . . . . The tragedy is that this organization receives funds and donations. As we hear of this terror attack, we must ask if the perpetrators were educated to become suicide bombers with funds originating with American and European taxpayers." Palazzi, a student of history as well as a holy man, went on to state the obvious: "It is necessary to fight terror in all its forms. If you promote a Palestinian state with American and European funds for the PLO, you increase the opportunity for terror."

Sheikh Palazzi contends that suicide bombing is an Islamic sin. He states, "Even if it involved the murder of no one else, a suicide is considered to shut the door to heaven." He asserts that targeting civilians for murder is totally unacceptable according to fundamental Islamic notions. He claims that the concept of martyrdom is alien to Islam when he says, "A martyr is someone who is killed despite his best efforts, not someone who commits suicide." He goes on to point out that the entire intifada is contrary to Islamic law, which considers rebellion against any state that does not prevent Muslims from worshipping freely or educating their children as "*fitneh*," or sedition. Echoing Emir Faisal, who expressed his convictions in the Faisal-Weizmann Agreement in 1919, Sheikh Palazzi states, "The ability to live in peace with Israel should represent the benchmark for judging whether an Arab state is prepared to accept democracy."

And what about the question of peace between the Palestinian Arabs west of the Jordan River and the Palestinian Jews of Israel? Don't the Palestinian Arabs, who, after all, are not Jewish, while Israel is a Jewish state, deserve some level of fulfillment of their national, political, and cultural aspirations? The simple and unavoidable answer to this question is yes. The solution to the question of Palestinian sovereignty is staring us right in the face, but no one wants to see it or dares to mention it. The solution was already arrived at back in 1921 and it can be encapsulated in a statement made by Dr. Kadri Toukan, the former Jordanian foreign minister, on December 9, 1970. That statement was, "Jordan is Palestine and Palestine is Jordan."

The sentiment was reiterated by Anwar Nusseibi, a former Jordanian defense minister, who stated on October 3, 1970: "The Jordanians are also Palestinians. This is one State. This is one people. The name is not important. The families living in Salt, Irbid, and Karak maintain not only family and matrimonial ties with the families in Nablus and Hebron, they are one people." Ahmad Shuqairy, the first president of the PLO, made the same observation when he told the Palestine National Council in May of 1965 that "Our Jordanian brothers are actually Palestinians."

The Washington, D.C., website of the Hashemite kingdom of Jordan says the following regarding the two Palestinian populations: "The . . . close historical and geographical relationship between Jordan and Palestine over the ages, together with . . . the national affiliation and cultural position of Jordanians and Palestinians . . . have endowed this relationship with a special and distinctive character. It is bolstered by the strong ties and deep common interests that exist between them."[2]

Yosef Tekoah, Israeli Ambassador to the United Nations, captured the essence of the question in a speech he delivered to the General Assembly on November 13, 1974:

No nation has enjoyed greater fulfillment of its political rights, no nation has been endowed with territory, sovereignty, and independence more abundantly, than the Arabs. Of common language, culture, religion, and origin, the Arab nation stormed out of its birth land in the seventh century and conquered one people after another until its rule encompassed the entire Arab peninsula, the Fertile Crescent, and North Africa. As a result of centuries of acquisition of territory by war, the Arab nation is represented in the United Nations by twenty sovereign States. Among them is also the Palestinian Arab State of Jordan. Geographically and ethnically Jordan is Palestine. Historically both the West and East Banks of the Jordan River are parts of the land of Israel or Palestine. The population of Jordan is composed of two elements—the sedentary population and nomads. Both are, of course, Palestinian. The nomad Bedouin constitute a minority of Jordan's population. Moreover, the majority of the sedentary inhabitants, even of the East Bank, are of Palestinian West Bank origin. Without the Palestinians, Jordan is a State without a people.

But what about the approximately two and a half million Palestinian Arabs living west of the Jordan River in a region presently under Israeli control? The regions of Samaria, Judea, and Gaza include cities and towns that are exclusively Arab, yet these population centers are presently controlled by Israel. The fact that Israel has agreed that these areas should be under Arab control numerous times in history and that Israel has been forced to exercise control over these areas out of concern for national survival is a separate matter. The point is that Israel, the national homeland for the Jewish people, cannot realistically continue to perpetually control a population that is not Jewish and that does not want to be controlled by a Jewish state. So, what should be done?

This is a question that has been pondered over by some of the best minds of the past one hundred years and I don't claim to be in their league. I can only throw in my two cents and, in doing so, I make no great claims to possessing any special insights. In presenting my opinion, I certainly don't claim to speak for anyone but myself as I humbly present my thesis.

Given the simple and irrefutable fact that Jordan is Palestine east of the Jordan River in every sense of the word, historically, culturally, politically, ethnically, and in every other manner, and given the fact that there is no difference whatsoever between the two Palestinian Arab populations, as they are one people residing on both banks of the Jordan River, the present sovereign Hashemite kingdom of Jordan should be invited to play a significant role in a settlement of the conflict. Israel should remain the Jewish Palestinian state with an Israeli Arab minority, Jordan should remain the exclusively Arab Palestinian state, and the two Palestinian states, Israel and Jordan, should jointly administer the West Bank and Gaza.

A joint and permanent commission of Israelis and Jordanians, with wide authority to govern, should be empanelled and charged with the responsibility of developing and maintaining overall military security and of disbanding terrorist militias and cells. Local and regional authorities should be created at the appropriate time, with elected mayors and legislators assuming control over local and regional matters. The Arabs of the West Bank and Gaza should be granted Jordanian citizenship and should look toward Amman as their political and cultural capital, while the Jews of the West Bank and Gaza should maintain Israeli citizenship and look toward Jerusalem. Both Israel and Jordan should strengthen their economic ties with each other and invest in the region.

As a long-term goal, Israel and Jordan should seriously consider forming an economic bloc together, with the European common market serving as a model. Economic integration and investment between the two Palestines, Israel, and Jordan, and joint investment in the shared Israel/Palestine condominium, Judea, Samaria, and Gaza, would go a long way toward eradicating vestiges of terror. There must be an overall denazification of the region, a ramping-down of incitement, and a reconstruction of the education system. No solution is ever going to make everyone happy, but given the long and bloody history of this conflict, a solution that involves a shared sovereignty is realistic and fair. The alternative is a yo-yo between Palestinian Arab control, followed by terror launched against Israel, and then followed by a costly military re-assertion of control of the region by Israel.

As far as the Golan Heights are concerned, Israel could consider negotiating over the future of the Golan on the condition that Syria is prepared to completely pull its forces out of Lebanon, that both Syria and Lebanon are prepared to eradicate their respective terrorist militias and cells, and that both nations are prepared to normalize their relations with Israel, which should include normal trade, travel across demilitarized frontiers, and all of the other features that constitute normal relations between bordering nations at peace with one another.

Sheikh Palazzi, in a speech he delivered in Rockland County, pointed out that many Arabs on the West Bank would prefer Israeli citizenship over that offered by a Palestinian state. While attending a conference in Jerusalem, Sheikh Palazzi recalled, he was approached by Arab residents of Jerusalem who told him that they would do anything to avoid being "sold out" to an Arafat regime. "They wanted to be recognized as Jordanian citizens with Jerusalem residency and did not want to become citizens of the oppressive Palestinian Authority," they told the visiting Sheikh. Sheikh Palazzi added, "If Arafat resigns and they get a new leader who is under his control, what good is that? If Arafat dies and the new leader simply continues his policies, what good is that? Children would still receive training in how to be suicide bombers."

Israeli Prime Minister Ariel Sharon accepted the principles outlined in the "roadmap to peace" presented by President George W. Bush, which called for an independent and sovereign Palestinian state on the West Bank and in Gaza. Like most people who are sick and tired of the genocidal campaign against the Jews of Israel, my hope and prayer is that this roadmap will be a success. There is no evidence to date, however, that any such state west of the Jordan River would be liberated from the strains of Nazism introduced by al-Husseini, nor does there appear to be a genuine will to change at this point from among the Palestinian Arab leadership.

In fact, after Israel withdrew from Gaza, including the evacuation of all Jews, Hamas won a majority in the PA legislature. Hamas is an off-shoot of the Muslim Brotherhood and calls for the total destruction of the State of Israel. After studying the life and times of Haj Amin al-Husseini, and after witnessing the evil fruits of that life, it grieves me to write that, at this juncture, my hopes and prayers for the success of the roadmap are mixed with more than a healthy dose of skepticism.

APPENDICES

Appendix A

The Balfour Declaration

Foreign Office, Nov. 2, 1917

Dear Lord Rothschild,

I have much pleasure in conveying to you, on behalf of His Majesty's Government, the following declaration of sympathy with Jewish Zionist aspirations which had been submitted to, and approved by, the Cabinet:

"His Majesty's Government views with favor the establishment in Palestine of a national home for the Jewish people, and will use their best endeavors to facilitate the achievement of this object, it being clearly understood that nothing shall be done which may prejudice the civil and religious rights of existing non-Jewish communities in Palestine, or the rights and political status enjoyed by Jews in any other country."

I should be grateful if you would bring this declaration to the knowledge of the Zionist Federation.

Yours sincerely,
Arthur James Balfour

Appendix B

The Faisal-Frankfurter Correspondence (excerpted)

Dear Mr. Frankfurter,

. . . We feel that the Arabs and Jews are cousins in race, having suffered similar oppressions at the hands of powers stronger than themselves, and by a happy coincidence have been able to take the first step toward the attainment of their national ideals together. We Arabs, especially the educated among us, look with the deepest sympathy on the Zionist movement. Our deputation here in Paris is fully acquainted with the proposals submitted yesterday by the Zionist Organization to the Peace Conference and we regard them as moderate and proper. We will do our best, in so far as we are concerned, to help them through. We will wish the Jews a most hearty welcome home.

. . . Dr. Weizmann has been a great helper of our cause, and I hope the Arabs may soon be in a position to make the Jews welcome in return for their kindness. We are working together on a reformed and revived Near East, and our two movements complete one another. The Jewish movement is national and not imperialist; our movement is national and not imperialist; and there is room in Syria for us both. Indeed, I think that neither can be a real success without the other.

People less informed and less reasonable than our leaders and yours, ignoring the need for co-operation of the Arabs and Zionists, have been trying to exploit the local difficulties that must necessarily arise in Palestine in the early stages of our movement. Some of them have, I am afraid, misrepresented your aims to the Arab peasantry and our aims to the Jewish peasantry with the result, that interested parties have been able to make capital out of what they call our differences.

. . . I look forward, and my people with me look forward, to a future in which we will help you and you will help us, so that the countries in which we are mutually interested may once again take their places in the community of civilized people of the world.

Believe me,
Yours sincerely,
FAISAL

Appendix C

The Weizmann-Faisal Agreement

January 1919

His Royal Highness the Emir FAISAL, representing and acting on behalf of the Arab Kingdom of HEJAZ, and Dr. Chiam Weizmann, representing and acting on behalf of the Zionist Organization, mindful of the racial kinship and ancient bonds existing between the Arabs and the Jewish people, and realizing that the surest means of working out the consummation of their national aspirations, is through the closest possible collaboration in the development of the Arab State and Palestine, and being desirous further of confirming the good understanding which exists between them, have agreed upon the following articles:

Article I

The Arab State and Palestine in their relations and undertakings shall be controlled by the most cordial goodwill and understanding and to this end Arab and Jewish duly accredited agents shall be established and maintained in their respective territories.

Article II

Immediately following the completion of deliberations of the Peace Conference, the definite boundaries between the Arab State and Palestine shall be determined by a commission to be agreed upon by the parties hereto.

Article III

In the establishment of the Constitution and Administration of Palestine all such measures shall be adopted as will afford the fullest guarantees for carrying into effect the British Government's Declaration of the 2nd of November 1917 [Balfour Declaration].

Article IV

All necessary measures will be taken to encourage and stimulate the immigration of Jews into Palestine on a large scale, and as quickly as possible to settle Jewish immigrants upon the land through closer settlement and intensive cultivation of the soil. In taking such measures the Arab peasants and tenant farmers shall be protected in their rights, and shall be assisted in forwarding their economic development.

Article V

No regulation or law shall be made prohibiting or interfering in any way with the free exercise of religion; and further the free exercise and expression of religious profession and worship without discrimination or preference shall forever be allowed. No religious test shall ever be required for the exercise of civil or religious rights.

Article VI

The Mohammedan Holy Places shall be under Mohammedan control.

Article VII

The Zionist Organization proposes to send to Palestine a commission of experts to make a survey of the economic possibilities of the country, and to report upon the best means for its development. The Zionist Organization will use its best efforts to assist the Arab in providing the means for developing the natural resources and economic possibilities thereof.

Article VIII

The parties hereto agree to act in complete accord and harmony in all matters embraced herein before the Peace Conference.

Article IX

Any matters of dispute, which may arise between the contracting parties, shall be referred to the British Government for arbitration.

Given under our hand at LONDON, ENGLAND, the THIRD day of JANUARY, ONE THOUSAND NINE HUNDRED AND NINETEEN.

Provided the Arabs obtain their independence as demanded in my memorandum dated the 4th of January, 1919, to the Foreign Office of the Government of Great Britain, I shall concur in the above articles.

But if the slightest departure or modification were to be made, I shall not then be bound by a single word of the present Agreement which shall be deemed void and of no account or validity, and I shall not be answerable in any way whatsoever.

FAISAL IBN HUSSEIN
CHAIM WEIZMANN

Appendix D

Palestine Royal Commission Report–
Peel Commission

Dialogue between Lord Peel and the Mufti

LORD PEEL: Since you demand the establishment of a national government in Palestine, what will you do with the 400,000 Jews already living there?

MUFTI: It will not be the first time that Jews have lived under the aegis of an Arab state. In the past it has been the Arab states which were the more compassionate to them. History shows that, during all periods, the Jews only found rest under the protection of Arab rulers. The East was always a shelter for Jews escaping from European pressure.

LORD PEEL: You stated that the number of Jews has increased steeply, so that the number of Arabs, which during the time of the conquest was approximately 90 percent of the total population, has now dropped to 70 percent.

MUFTI: That is correct.

LORD PEEL: Notwithstanding this, if you reach agreement with the English, will you be prepared to allow the Jews to remain in the country?

MUFTI: That is a matter for the government that will be formed to deal with at the appropriate time. Its principle will be justice, and above all else it will concern itself with the interests and benefit of the country.

LORD PEEL: Do you think that the Jews will accept this declaration without receiving something more substantial? Such an oral declaration will not convince them.

MUFTI: Jews living in the other Arab states currently enjoy freedoms and rights.

LORD PEEL: I feel that I can safely assume what the Jews will have to say on this matter.

QUESTION: Does his Eminence think that this country can assimilate and digest the 400,000 Jews now in this country?

ANSWER: No

QUESTION: Some of them would have to be removed by a process kindly or painful as the case may be?

ANSWER: We must leave all this to the future.

Comments in the final committee report: We are not questioning the sincerity or the humanity of the Mufti's intentions and those of his colleagues, but we cannot forget what recently happened, despite treaty provisions and explicit assurances, to the Assyrian minority in Iraq; nor can we forget that the hatred of the Arab politician for the National Home has never been concealed and that it has now permeated the Arab population as a whole.

Appendix E

Minutes of the meeting with Hitler and Amin al-Husseini

Source: *Documents on German Foreign Policy 1918-1945*, Series D, Vol XIII, London, 1964, pp.881 ff.

German Chancellor Adolf Hitler and grand mufti Haj Amin al-Husseini: Zionism and the Arab cause (November 28, 1941)

Haj Amin al-Husseini, the most influential leader of Palestinian Arabs, lived in Germany during the Second World War. He met Hitler, Ribbentrop, and other Nazi leaders on various occasions and attempted to coordinate Nazi and Arab policies in the Middle East.

Record of the conversation between the Führer and the Grand Mufti of Jerusalem on November 28th, 1941, in the presence of Reich Foreign Minister and Minister Grobba in Berlin.

The Grand Mufti began by thanking the Führer for the great honor he had bestowed by receiving him. He wished to seize the opportunity to convey to the Führer of the Greater German Reich, admired by the entire Arab world, his thanks for the sympathy, which he has always shown for the Arab and especially the Palestinian cause, and to which he had given clear expression in his public speeches. The Arab countries were firmly convinced that Germany would win the war and that the Arab cause would then prosper. The Arabs were Germany's natural friends because they had the same enemies as had Germany, namely the English, the Jews, and the Communists. Therefore they were prepared to cooperate with Germany with all their hearts and stood ready to participate in the war, not only negatively by the commission of acts of sabotage and the instigation of revolutions, but also positively by the formation of an Arab Legion. The Arabs could be more useful to Germany as allies than might be apparent at first glance, both for geographical reasons and because of the suffering inflicted on them by the English and the Jews. Furthermore, they had had close relations with all

Moslem nations, of which they could make use on behalf of the common cause. The Arab Legion would be quite easy to rise. An appeal by the Mufti to the Arab countries and the prisoners of the Arab, Algerian, Tunisian, and Moroccan nationality in Germany would produce a great number of volunteers eager to fight. Of Germany's victory the allied world was firmly convinced, not only because the Reich possessed a large army, brave soldiers, and military leaders of genius, but also because the Almighty could never award a victory to an unjust cause.

In this struggle, the Arabs were striving for the independence and unity of Palestine, Syria and Iraq. They had the fullest confidence in the Führer and looked to his hand for the balm on their wounds, which had been inflicted upon them by the enemies of Germany.

The Mufti then mentioned the letter he had received from Germany, which stated that Germany was holding no Arab territories and understood and recognized the aspirations to independence and freedom of the Arabs, just as she supported the elimination of the Jewish national home.

A public declaration in this sense would be very useful for its propagandistic effect on the Arab peoples at this moment. It would rouse the Arabs from their momentary lethargy and give them new courage. It would also ease the Mufti's work of secretly organizing the Arabs against the moment when they could strike. At the same time, he could give the assurance that the Arabs would in strict discipline patiently wait for the right moment and only strike upon an order from Berlin.

With regard to events in Iraq, the Mufti observed that the Arabs in that country certainly had by no means been incited by Germany to attack England, but solely had acted in reaction to a direct English assault upon their honor.

The Turks, he believed, would welcome the establishment of an Arab government in the neighboring territories because they would prefer weaker Arab to strong European governments in the neighboring countries and, being themselves a nation of 7 million, they had moreover nothing to fear from the 1,700,000 Arabs inhabiting Syria, Transjordan, Iraq, and Palestine.

France likewise would have no objections to the unification plan because she had conceded independence to Syria as early as 1936 and had given her approval to the unification of Iraq and Syria under King Faisal as early as 1933.

In these circumstances he was renewing his request that the Führer make a public declaration so that the Arabs would not lose hope, which is so powerful a force in the life of nations. With such hope in their hearts the Arabs, as he had said, were willing to wait. They were not pressing for the immediate realization of their aspirations; they could easily wait half a year or a whole year. But if they were not inspired with such a hope by a declaration of this sort, it could be expected that the English would be the gainers from it.

The Führer replied that Germany's fundamental attitude on these questions, as the Mufti himself had already stated, was clear. Germany stood for uncompromising war against the Jews. That naturally included active opposition to the Jewish national home in Palestine, which was nothing other than a center, in the form of a state, for the exercise of destructive influence by Jewish interests. Germany was also aware that the assertion that the Jews were carrying out the functions of economic pioneers in Palestine was a lie. The work there was done only by Arabs, not by Jews. Germany was resolved, step by step, to ask one European nation after the other to solve its Jewish problem, and at the proper time to direct a similar appeal to non-European nations as well.

Germany was at the present time engaged in a life or death struggle with two citadels of Jewish power, Great Britain and Soviet Russia. Theoretically, there was a difference between England's capitalism and Soviet Russia's communism; actually, however, the Jews in both countries were pursuing a common goal. This was the decisive struggle; on the political plane, it presented itself in the main as a conflict between Germany and England, but ideologically it was a battle between National Socialism and the Jews. It went without saying that Germany would furnish positive and practical aid to the Arabs involved in the same struggle, because platonic promises were useless in a war for survival or destruction in which the Jews were able to mobilize all of England's power for their ends.

The aid to the Arabs would have to be material aid. Of how little help sympathies alone were in such a battle has been demonstrated plainly by the operation in Iraq, where circumstances had not permitted the rendering of really effective, practical aid. In spite of all the sympathies, German aid had not been sufficient and Iraq was overcome by the power of Britain, that is, the guardian of the Jews.

The Mufti could not be aware, however, that the outcome of the struggle going on at present would also decide the fate of the Arab world. The Führer had to think and speak coolly and deliberately, as a rational man and primarily as a soldier, as the leader of the German and allied armies. Everything of a nature to help in this titanic battle for the common cause, and thus also for the Arabs, would have to be done. Anything however, that might contribute to weakening the military situation must be put aside, no matter how unpopular this move might be.

Germany was now engaged in very severe battles to force the gateway to the northern Caucasus region. The difficulties were mainly with regard to maintaining the supply, which was most difficult as a result of the destruction of railroads and highways as well as the oncoming winter. If at such a moment, the Führer were to raise the problem of Syria in a declaration, those elements in France which were under DeGaulle's influence would receive new strength. They would interpret the Führer's declaration as an intention to break up France's colonial empire and appeal to their fellow countrymen that they should rather make common cause with the English to try to save what still could be saved. A German declaration regarding Syria would in France be understood to refer to the French colonies in general, and that would at the present time create new troubles in western Europe, which means that a portion of the German armed forces would be immobilized in the west and no longer available for the campaign in the east.

The Führer than made the following statement to the Mufti, enjoining him to lock it in the uttermost depths of his heart.

1. He (the Führer) would carry on the battle to the total destruction of the Judeo-Communist empire in Europe.
2. At some moment which was impossible to set exactly today but which in any event was not distant, the German armies would in the course of this struggle reach the southern exit from Caucasia.
3. As soon as this had happened, the Führer would on his own give the Arab the assurance that its hour of liberation had arrived. Germany's objective would then be solely the destruction of the Jewish element residing in the Arab sphere under the protection of British power. In that hour the Mufti would be the most authoritative spokesman for the Arab world. It would

then be his task to set off the Arab operations, which he had secretly prepared. When that time had come, Germany could also be indifferent to French reaction to such a declaration.

Once Germany had forced open the road to Iran and Iraq through Rostov; it would also be the beginning of the end of the British world empire. He (the Führer) hoped that the coming year would make it possible for Germany to thrust open the Caucasian gate to the Middle East. For the good of their common cause, it would be better if the Arab proclamation were put off for a few more months than if Germany were to create difficulties for herself without being able to thereby help the Arabs.

He (the Führer) fully appreciated the eagerness of the Arabs for a public declaration of the sort requested by the grand mufti. But he would beg him to consider that he (the Führer) himself was the Chief of State of the German Reich for five long years during which he was unable to make to his own homeland the announcement of its liberation. He had to wait with that until the announcement could be made on the basis of a situation brought about by the force of arms that the Anschluss had been carried out.

The moment that Germany's tank divisions and air squadrons had made their appearance south of the Caucasus, the public appeal requested by the Grand Mufti could go out to the Arab world.

The Grand Mufti replied that it was his view that everything would come to pass just as the Führer had indicated. He was fully reassured and satisfied by the words which he had heard from the Chief of the German State. He asked, however, whether it would not be possible, secretly at least, to enter into an agreement with Germany of the kind he had just outlined for the Führer.

The Führer replied that he had just now given the Grand Mufti precisely that confidential declaration.

The Grand Mufti thanked him for it and stated in conclusion that he was taking his leave from the Führer in full confidence and with reiterated thanks for the interest shown in the Arab cause.

SCHMIDT

Appendix F

This is excerpted from the diary of Haj Amin al-Husseini, recorded in his own handwriting, on his meeting with Hitler.

The Arab Higher Committee—The Documentary Record

The words of the Führer on the 6th of Zul Qaada 1360 of the Hejira [which falls on the 21st of November 1941] Berlin, Friday, from 4:30 P.M. till a few minutes after 6. The objectives of my fight are clear. Primarily, I am fighting the Jews without respite, and this fight includes the fight against the so-called Jewish National Home in Palestine because the Jews want to establish there a central government for their own pernicious purposes, and to undertake a devastating and ruinous expansion at the expense of the governments of the world and of other peoples.

It is clear that the Jews have accomplished nothing in Palestine and their claims are lies. All the accomplishments in Palestine are due to the Arabs and not to the Jews. I am resolved to find a solution for the Jewish problem, progressing step by step without cessation. With regard to this I am making the necessary and right appeal, first to all the European countries and then to countries outside of Europe.

It is true that our common enemies are Great Britain and the Soviets whose principles are opposed to ours. But behind them stands hidden Jewry, which drives them both. Jewry has but one aim in both these countries. We are now in the midst of a life and death struggle against both these nations. This fight will not only determine the outcome of the struggle between National Socialism and Jewry, but the whole conduct of this successful war will be of great and positive help to the Arabs who are engaged in the same struggle.

This is not only an abstract assurance. A mere promise would be of no value whatsoever. But assurance, which rests upon a conquering force, is the only one, which has real value. In the Iraqi campaign, for instance, the sympathy of the whole German people was for Iraq. It was our aim to help Iraq, but circumstances prevented us from furnishing actual help. The German people saw in them [in the

Iraqis] comrades in suffering because the German people too have suffered as they have. All the help we gave Iraq was not sufficient to save Iraq from the British forces. For this reason it is necessary to underscore one thing: in this struggle which will decide the fate of the Arabs I can now speak as a man dedicated to an ideal and as a military leader and a soldier. Everyone united in this great struggle who helps to bring about its successful outcome, serves the common cause and thus serves the Arab cause. Any other view means weakening the military situation and thus offers no help to the Arab cause. Therefore it is necessary for us to decide the steps which can help us against world Jewry, against Communist Russia and England, and which among them can be most useful. Only if we win the war will the hour of deliverance also be the hour of fulfillment of Arab aspirations.

The situation is as follows: We are conducting the great struggle to open the way to the North of the Caucasus. The difficulties involved are more than transportation because of the demolished railways and roads and because of winter weather. And if I venture in these circumstances to issue a declaration with regard to Syria, then the pro-de Gaulle elements in France will be strengthened and this might cause a revolt in France. These men [the French] will be convinced then that joining Britain is more advantageous and the detachment of Syria is a pattern to be followed in the remainder of the French Empire. This will strengthen de Gaulle's stand in the colonies. If the declaration is issued now, difficulties will arise in Western Europe, which will cause the diversion of some [German] forces for defensive purposes, thus preventing us from sending all our forces to the East.

Now I am going to tell you something I would like you to keep secret. First, I will keep up my fight until the complete destruction of the Judeo-Bolshevik rule has been accomplished.

Second, during the struggle (and we don't know when victory will come, but probably not in the far future) we will reach the Southern Caucasus.

Third, then I would like to issue a declaration; for then the hour of the liberation of the Arabs will have arrived. Germany has no ambitions in this area but cares only to annihilate the power, which produces the Jews.

Fourth, I am happy that you have escaped and that you are now with the Axis powers. The hour will strike when you will be the lord of the supreme word and not only the conveyer of our declarations. You will be the man to direct the Arab force and at that moment I cannot imagine what would happen to the Western peoples.

Fifth, I think that with this Arab advance begins the dismemberment of the British world. The road from Rostov to Iran and Iraq is shorter than the distance from Berlin to Rostov. We hope next year to smash this barrier. It is better then and not now that a declaration should be issued as (now) we cannot help in anything.

I understand the Arab desire for this [declaration], but His Excellency the Mufti must understand that only five years after I became President of the German government and Führer of the German people, was I able to get such a declaration [the Austrian Union], and this because military forces prevented me from issuing such a declaration. But when the German Panzer tanks and the German air squadrons reach the Southern Caucasus, then will be the time to issue the declaration.

He said [in reply to a request that a secret declaration or a treaty be made] that a declaration known to a number of persons cannot remain secret but will become public. I [Hitler] have made very few declarations in my life, unlike the British who have made many declarations. If I issue a declaration, I will uphold it. Once I promised the Finnish Marshal that I would help his country if the enemy attacks again. This word of mine made a stronger impression than any written declaration.

Recapitulating, I want to state the following to you: When we shall have arrived in the Southern Caucasus, then the time of the liberation of the Arabs will have arrived. And you can rely on my word.

We were troubled about you. I know your life history. I followed with interest your long and dangerous journey. I was very concerned about you. I am happy that you are with us now and that you are now in a position to add your strength to the common cause.

Appendix G

Mufti asks Hungary to send Jews to Poland

Rome
June 28, 1943

His Excellency
The Minister of Foreign Affairs for Hungary

Your Excellency,

You no doubt know of the struggle between the Arabs and Jews of Palestine, that it has been and what it is, a long and bloody fight, brought about by the desire of the Jews to create a national home, a Jewish state in the near east, with the help and protection of England and the United States. In fact, behind it lies the hope, which the Jews have never relinquished, namely, the domination of the whole world through this important, strategic center, Palestine. In effect their program has among other purposes, always aimed at the encouragement of Jewish migration to Palestine and the other countries of the near east. However, the war, as well as the understanding which the members of the Three-Power-Pact of the responsibility of the Jews for its outbreak and finally their evil intentions toward these countries which protected them until now—all these are reasons for placing them under such vigilant control as will definitely stop their emigration to Palestine or elsewhere.

Lately I have been informed of the uninterrupted efforts made by the English and the Jews to obtain permission for the Jews living in your country to leave for Palestine via Bulgaria and Turkey.

I have also learned that these negotiations were successful since some of the Jews of Hungary have had the satisfaction of emigrating to Palestine via Bulgaria and Turkey and that a group of these Jews arrived in Palestine last March. The Jewish Agency, which supervises the execution of the Jewish program, has published a bulletin, which contains important information on the current negotiations between the English government and the governments of other interested states to send the Jews of Balkan countries to Palestine. The Jewish Agency quoted, among other things, its receipt of a sufficient number of immigration certificates for 900 Jewish children to be transported from Hungary, accompanied by 100 adults.

To authorize these Jews to leave your country under the above circumstances and in this way, would by no means solve the Jewish problem and would certainly not protect your country against their evil influence—far from it!—for the escape would make it possible for them to communicate and combine freely with their racial brethren in enemy countries in order to strengthen their position and to exert a more dangerous influence on the outcome of the war, especially since, as a consequence of their long stay in your country, they are necessarily in a position to know many of your secrets and also about your war effort. All this comes on top of the terrible damage done to the friendly Arab nation which has taken its place at your side in this war and which cherishes for your country the most sincere feelings and the very best wishes.

This is the reason why I ask your excellency to permit me to draw your attention to the necessity of preventing the Jews from leaving your country for Palestine: and if there are reasons which make their removal necessary, it would be indispensable and infinitely preferable to send them to other countries where they would find themselves under active control, for example, in Poland, in order thereby to protect oneself from their menace and avoid the consequent damages.

Yours etc.

Appendix H

Mufti Address to Arab-Americans

Excerpted from a radio address by the mufti, March 19, 1943—
Rome. Source: *The Arab War Effort: A Documented Account.*

The Arabs and Moslems will not be deceived by Britain once again
because not only have they known its true intentions but they have
also known those of Britain's allies—America—and I want to draw
the attention of the Arab emigrants in America to this fact, reminding them of their glorious past when they supported the National
movement. I would also like to remind them that their efforts will
be wasted if, God forbid, America and her Allies may be victorious
in this War because at such a time the Arabs will never rise again.
I therefore know that those Arab emigrants in America will refrain
from helping Roosevelt or taking part in a war, which he brought on
to his country.

If those allies win this war the Jewish influence will be the arbiter
in the world resources and one can thus imagine the future of the Arabs and Moslems, and the dangers which they are exposed to in their
fatherlands and beliefs if the Jews and their allies dominate them and
spread the latent hatred on to them.

Then the world will become Hell—God forbid: but Allah is too
just and merciful to grant such murderous violators any victory. We
are sure that victory will be ours and that of our friends. We have not
the slightest doubt about that, we shall not slacken our struggle nor
will we be deterred or questioned. Do not be deceived by the allegations
of your enemies, because you know full well about their intrigues,
and be sure that the nation, which fights, sacrifices and waits, will be
the victorious one in the end.

Appendix I

The Palestinian National Covenant

Article 1. Palestine is the homeland of the Arab Palestinian people; it is an indivisible part of the Arab homeland, and the Palestinian people are an integral part of the Arab nation.

Article 2. Palestine, with the boundaries it had during the British Mandate is an indivisible territorial unit.

Article 3. The Palestinian Arab people possess the legal right to their homeland and have the right to determine their destiny after achieving the liberation of their country in accordance with their wishes and entirely of their own accord and will.

Article 4. The Palestinian identity is a genuine, essential, and inherent characteristic; it is transmitted from parents to children. The Zionist occupation and the dispersal of the Palestinian Arab people, through the disasters, which befell them, do not make them lose their Palestinian identity and their membership in the Palestinian community, nor do they negate them.

Article 5. The Palestinians are those Arab nationals who, until 1947, normally resided in Palestine regardless of whether they were evicted from it or have stayed there. Anyone born, after that date, of a Palestinian father—whether inside Palestine or outside it—is also a Palestinian.

Article 6. The Jews who had normally resided in Palestine until the beginning of the Zionist invasion will be considered Palestinians.

Article 7. That there is a Palestinian community and that it has material, spiritual, and historical connection with Palestine are indisputable facts. It is a national duty to bring up individual Palestinians in an Arab revolutionary manner. All means of information and education must be adopted in order to acquaint the Palestinian with his country in the most profound manner, both spiritual and material, that is possible. He must be prepared for the armed struggle and ready to sacrifice his wealth and his life in order to win back his homeland and bring about its liberation.

Article 8. The phase in their history, through which the Palestinian people are now living, is that of national [watani] struggle for the liberation of Palestine. Thus the conflicts among the Palestinian national forces are secondary, and should be ended for the sake of the basic conflict that exists between the forces of Zionism and of imperialism on the one hand, and the Palestinian Arab people on the other. On this basis the Palestinian masses, regardless of whether they are residing in the national homeland or in diaspora [mahajir] constitute—both their organizations and the individuals—one national front working for the retrieval of Palestine and its liberation through armed struggle.

Article 9. Armed struggle is the only way to liberate Palestine. This is the overall strategy, not merely a tactical phase. The Palestinian Arab people assert their absolute determination and firm resolution to continue their armed struggle and to work for an armed popular revolution for the liberation of their country and their return to it. They also assert their right to normal life in Palestine and to exercise their right to self-determination and sovereignty over it.

Article 10. Commando action constitutes the nucleus of the Palestinian popular liberation war. This requires its escalation, comprehensiveness, and the mobilization of all the Palestinian popular and educational efforts and their organization and involvement in the armed Palestinian revolution. It also requires the achieving of unity for the national [watani] struggle among the different groupings of the Palestinian people, and between the Palestinian people and the Arab masses, so as to secure the continuation of the revolution, its escalation, and victory.

Article 11. The Palestinians will have three mottoes: national [wataniyya] unity, national [qawmiyya] mobilization, and liberation.

Article 12. The Palestinian people believe in Arab unity. In order to contribute their share toward the attainment of that objective, however, they must, at the present stage of their struggle, safeguard their

Palestinian identity and develop their consciousness of that identity, and oppose any plan that may dissolve or impair it.

Article 13. Arab unity and the liberation of Palestine are two complementary objectives, the attainment of either of which facilitates the attainment of the other. Thus, Arab unity leads to the liberation of Palestine, the liberation of Palestine leads to Arab unity; and work toward the realization of one objective proceeds side by side with work toward the realization of the other.

Article 14. The destiny of the Arab nation, and indeed Arab existence itself, depend upon the destiny of the Palestine cause. From this interdependence springs the Arab nation's pursuit of, and striving for, the liberation of Palestine. The people of Palestine play the role of the vanguard in the realization of this sacred [qawmi] goal.

Article 15. The liberation of Palestine, from an Arab viewpoint, is a national [qawmi] duty and it attempts to repel the Zionist and imperialist aggression against the Arab homeland, and aims at the elimination of Zionism in Palestine. Absolute responsibility for this falls upon the Arab nation—peoples and governments—with the Arab people of Palestine in the vanguard. Accordingly, the Arab nation must mobilize all its military, human, moral, and spiritual capabilities to participate actively with the Palestinian people in the liberation of Palestine. It must, particularly in the phase of the armed Palestinian revolution, offer and furnish the Palestinian people with all possible help, and material and human support, and make available to them the means and opportunities that will enable them to continue to carry out their leading role in the armed revolution, until they liberate their homeland.

Article 16. The liberation of Palestine, from a spiritual point of view, will provide the Holy Land with an atmosphere of safety and tranquility, which in turn will safeguard the country's religious sanctuaries and guarantee freedom of worship and of visit to all, without discrimination of race, color, language, or religion. Accordingly, the people of Palestine look to all spiritual forces in the world for support.

Article 17. The liberation of Palestine, from a human point of view, will restore to the Palestinian individual his dignity, pride, and freedom. Accordingly the Palestinian Arab people look forward to the support of all those who believe in the dignity of man and his freedom in the world.

Article 18. The liberation of Palestine, from an international point of view, is a defensive action necessitated by the demands of self-defense. Accordingly the Palestinian people, desirous as they are of the friendship of all people, look to freedom-loving, and peace-loving states for support in order to restore their legitimate rights in Palestine, to re-establish peace and security in the country, and to enable its people to exercise national sovereignty and freedom.

Article 19. The Partition of Palestine in 1947 and the establishment of the state of Israel are entirely illegal, regardless of the passage of time, because they were contrary to the will of the Palestinian people and to their natural right in their homeland, and inconsistent with the principles embodied in the Charter of the United Nations; particularly the right to self-determination.

Article 20. The Balfour Declaration, the Mandate for Palestine, and everything that has been based upon them, are deemed null and void. Claims of historical or religious ties of Jews with Palestine are incompatible with the facts of history and the true conception of what constitutes statehood. Judaism, being a religion, is not an independent nationality. Nor do Jews constitute a single nation with an identity of its own; they are citizens of the states to which they belong.

Article 21. The Arab Palestinian people, expressing themselves by the armed Palestinian revolution, reject all solutions which are substitutes for the total liberation of Palestine and reject all proposals aiming at the liquidation of the Palestinian problem, or its internationalization.

Article 22. Zionism is a political movement organically associated with international imperialism and antagonistic to all action for liberation and to progressive movements in the world. It is racist and fanatic in its nature, aggressive, expansionist, and colonial in its aims, and fascist in its methods. Israel is the instrument of the Zionist movement, and geographical base for world imperialism placed strategically in the midst of the Arab homeland to combat the hopes of the Arab nation for liberation, unity, and progress. Israel is a constant source of threat vis-à-vis peace in the Middle East and the whole world. Since the liberation of Palestine will destroy the Zionist and imperialist presence and will contribute to the establishment of peace in the Middle East, the Palestinian people look for the support of all the progressive and peaceful forces and urge them all, irrespective of their affiliations and beliefs, to offer the Palestinian people all aid and support in their just struggle for the liberation of their homeland.

Article 23. The demand of security and peace, as well as the demand of right and justice, require all states to consider Zionism an illegitimate movement, to outlaw its existence, and to ban its operations, in order that friendly relations among peoples may be preserved, and the loyalty of citizens to their respective homelands safeguarded.

Article 24. The Palestinian people believe in the principles of justice, freedom, sovereignty, self-determination, human dignity, and in the right of all peoples to exercise them.

Article 25. For the realization of the goals of this Charter and its principles, the Palestine Liberation Organization will perform its role in the liberation of Palestine in accordance with the Constitution of this Organization.

Article 26. The Palestine Liberation Organization, representative of the Palestinian revolutionary forces, is responsible for the Palestinian Arab people's movement in its struggle—to retrieve its homeland, liberate and return to it and exercise the right to self-determination in it—in all military, political, and financial fields and also for whatever may be required by the Palestine case on the inter-Arab and international levels.

Article 27. The Palestine Liberation Organization shall cooperate with all Arab states, each according to its potentialities; and will adopt a neutral policy among them in the light of the requirements of the war of liberation; and on this basis it shall not interfere in the internal affairs of any Arab state.

Article 28. The Palestinian Arab people assert the genuineness and independence of their national [wataniyya] revolution and reject all forms of intervention, trusteeship, and subordination.

Article 29. The Palestinian people possess the fundamental and genuine legal right to liberate and retrieve their homeland. The Palestinian people determine their attitude toward all states and forces on the basis of the stands they adopt vis-à-vis to the Palestinian revolution to fulfill the aims of the Palestinian people.

Article 30. Fighters and carriers of arms in the war of liberation are the nucleus of the popular army, which will be the protective force for the gains of the Palestinian Arab people.

Article 31. The Organization shall have a flag, an oath of allegiance, and an anthem. All this shall be decided upon in accordance with a special regulation.

Article 32. Regulations, which shall be known as the Constitution of the Palestinian Liberation Organization, shall be annexed to this Charter. It will lay down the manner in which the Organization, and its organs and institutions, shall be constituted; the respective competence of each; and the requirements of its obligation under the Charter.

Article 33. This Charter shall not be amended save by [vote of] a majority of two-thirds of the total membership of the National Congress of the Palestine Liberation Organization [taken] at a special session convened for that purpose.

The Nazi Connection to Islamic Terrorism

Speech delivered at the National Synagogue—Washington, D.C.—Jan. 18, 2006, as part of the program sponsored by Holocaust Museum Watch entitled "Should Arab Anti-Semitism Be on the US Holocaust Memorial Museum's Agenda?"

The thesis of my book is that modern Islamic terrorism is connected to Hitler's Nazism and that Hitler's biggest advocate was Haj Amin al-Husseini, the grand mufti of Jerusalem. I contrast the mufti, who introduced terror in Palestine in 1920 with a slaughter of Jewish settlers, and his contemporary, the enlightened King Faisal, who became the Hashemite king of Iraq. Faisal signed a treaty with Zionist leader Chaim Weizmann in 1919, which recognized Palestine as a Jewish state.

Faisal's view, along with that of his brother Abdallah, king of Jordan, whose great-grandson is the present king of Jordan, was not atypical in the Arab world in the early part of the twentieth century.

After al-Husseini instigated the 1920 pogrom against the Jews of Palestine, Herbert Samuel, the British administrator of Palestine and himself a Jew, appointed him as grand mufti of Jerusalem. This act of appeasement by Samuel finds its echoes in the response by many liberal world leaders to today's terrorist threat. The mufti proceeded to purge moderate Arabs from Palestine. In the 1920s, he used suicide bombers against moderate Arabs.

In 1937, the mufti met Nazi official Adolf Eichmann and was subsequently added to the Nazi payroll, according to testimony at the Nuremberg and Eichmann trials. After launching the 1937–1939 riots in Palestine, the mufti went to Iraq, where he played a key role in a pro-Nazi generals' coup in 1941. One of the pro-Nazi generals involved in the coup was the uncle and mentor of Saddam Hussein.

After the pro-Nazi Iraq coup failed, the mufti fled to Nazi Germany, where Hitler set him up as a Nazi-Muslim head of state in exile. From Berlin, living in a mansion confiscated from a Jew, the mufti was given access by the Nazis to the *Sonderfund*, which was money confiscated from the Jews of Germany. The mufti used the looted properties to spread anti-Semitic propaganda in the Middle East.

During the war, the mufti conducted anti-Semitic broadcasts, toured the death camps, and urged Eichmann, in a letter, to not spare thousands of Jewish children from the crematoria, reminding Eichmann that little Jews grow into big Jews. He urged the pro-Nazi governments of Hungary and Romania to send their Jews to Auschwitz and he supervised the pro-Nazi Muslim Hanzar brigades.

After the war the mufti fled to Cairo, where he played a major role in the war against Israeli independence in 1948 and was implicated in the assassination of King Abdallah of Jordan, Faisal's brother, who was about to sign a peace treaty with Israel. The mufti was involved in Operation Odessa, which settled Nazi war criminals in Arab countries. The mufti helped funnel Nazi loot into the Middle East, where the funds were applied toward the development of terror cells. Yasir Arafat, said by many to be the mufti's nephew, started out as a munitions procurer for the mufti's irregulars in the 1948 war. In his last public act, the mufti urged, at an Arab conference, that indigenous Jews still living in Arab countries be eliminated.

The U.S. Holocaust Museum has not adequately researched the issue of the origins of radical Islamic anti-Semitism. Perhaps this is because the museum is concerned over the possibility that such an investigation might be perceived as anti-Arab or anti-Muslim. Such a concern makes about as much sense as a suggestion that it would be anti-German to research Nazism or anti-Russian to research Soviet Communism. An investigation of radical Islamic anti-Semitism has nothing to do with race, ethnicity, nationality, or religion, but rather deals with a malevolent set of ideas that, when left unchecked, are capable of manifesting themselves in the form of a Holocaust.

The U.S. Holocaust Museum seeks to be more than just a repository of mementos to be viewed under glass and, in this regard, the museum has done good and important work exposing holocausts in Rwanda and in the Sudanese providence of Darfur.

However, the objectivity, not to mention the moral authority, of the Holocaust Museum is seriously eroded by this apparent unwillingness to highlight the slow-motion holocaust that is presently underway in the Islamic world. This holocaust is directed not only against the Jews of Israel, but also against indigenous Christian populations in Egypt, Lebanon, and elsewhere, against non-Muslim minorities, and against moderate Muslims.

The U. S. Holocaust Museum ought to be drawing a connection between this ongoing persecution and the recent and unprovoked slaughter of innocent people by Islamic extremists in non-Muslim centers such as Bali, Madrid, and London, as well as the carnage that occurred in New York, and in this great city of Washington, D.C., on September 11, 2001.

When the U.S. Holocaust Museum is silent in the face of radical Islamic anti-Semitism and terrorism they are aiding and abetting the enemies of peace and progress. This policy is particularly egregious at a time when President George W. Bush is demonstrating courageous leadership in the war against radical Islamic tyranny in Afghanistan and Iraq.

At a time when millions of Muslim Iraqis are risking their lives to vote, when Lebanese citizens are challenging the iron grip of their Syrian warlords, when Libya is disavowing nuclear weapons, the Holocaust Museum should be standing solidly with the moderate forces of freedom and progress in the Islamic world. I call upon the Holocaust Museum to live up to its own stated raison d'être.

Faisal, the enlightened king of Iraq, represents the progressive view that the existence of a small Jewish state benefits the Arab states in their quest for sovereignty and modernity. The mufti represents a regressive blend of Islam and National Socialism that remains the driving force behind Al Qaeda, Hizbollah, and Hamas.

The mufti found a soulmate in Hitler and carried Hitler's legacy into the Arab world. Many Western leaders, in the tradition of Herbert Samuel, continue to support policies that inadvertently aid the terrorists and hurt the moderates. However well intentioned these leaders might be, there is no room for mistakes in these dangerous times.

I call on the U.S. Holocaust Museum to put its considerable resources toward researching this history. A full reckoning of the truth will help the forces that seek to assist Arabs and Muslims in their quest to restore the better traditions of Islam and will help to stave off a potential holocaust. This research would go a long way toward putting teeth into the slogan "never again."

Prayer for the State of Israel–
The Chief Rabbinate

Our Father Who art in Heaven, Protector and Redeemer of Israel, bless Thou the State of Israel which marks the dawn of our deliverance. Shield it beneath the wings of Thy love; spread over it Thy canopy of peace; send Thy light and Thy truth to its leaders, officers, and counselors, and direct them with Thy good counsel.

O G-d, strengthen the defenders of our Holy Land; grant them salvation and crown them with victory. Establish peace in the land, and everlasting joy for its inhabitants.

Remember our brethren, the whole house of Israel, in all the lands of their dispersion. Speedily let them walk upright to Zion, the city, to Jerusalem Thy dwelling-place, as it is written in the Torah of Thy servant Moses: "Even if you are dispersed in the uttermost parts of the world, from there the L-rd your G-d will gather and fetch you. The L-rd your G-d will bring you into the land which your fathers possessed, and you shall possess it."

Unite our heart to love and revere Thy Name, and to observe all the precepts of Thy Torah. Shine forth in Thy glorious majesty over all the inhabitants of Thy world. Let everything that breathes proclaim: "The L-rd G-d of Israel is King; His majesty rules over all." Amen.

Sources

Adolf Hitler, *Mein Kampf* (New York: Houghton Mifflin, 1969).

Alan Dershowitz, *The Case for Israel* (Hoboken, New Jersey: John Wiley and Sons, 2003).

Arie Stav, "Arabs and Nazism." *Natav*, Nov. 1995.

Ben Hecht, *Perfidy* (New London, New Hampshire: Milah Press, 1997).

Benny Morris, The Birth of the Palestinian Refugee Problem, 1947–1949 (Cambridge: Cambridge University Press, 1989).

Benny Morris, *Righteous Victims: A History of the Zionist-Arab Conflict, 1881–2001* (New York: Alfred A. Knopf, 1999).

Bernard Lewis, *What Went Wrong? The Clash Between Islam and Modernity in the Middle East* (New York: Oxford University Press, 2002), 31.

Carl Savich, "Islam Under the Swastika." *Serbiana*, www.serbianna.com/columns/savich/022.shtml.

Council on Foreign Relations, "Terrorism: Questions and Answers."

Daniel Pipes, "If I Forget Thee: Does Jerusalem Really Matter to Islam?" New Republic, April 28, 1997.

David Lee Preston, "Hitler's Swiss Connection." *Philadelphia Enquirer*, January 5, 1997.

Embassy of Jordan, www.jordanembassyus.org/new/aboutjordan/national character.shtml#7.

Hitler's Friends in the Middle East, Weiner Library Bulletin, vol. XV (1961), 35.

H.R.Trevor-Roper, *Hitler: Secret Conversations*, (New York: Farrar, Strauss and Young, 1953), 512.

Israel State Archives (ISA), 79/18/A3024.

Israel State Archives (ISA), 79/12/A3017.

Israel State Archives (ISA), 79/12/A3024.

Ithamar Marcus, "Nazi Ally, Hajj Amin al-Husseini Is Arafat's Hero." *Palestine Media Watch*, August 5, 2002.

John Rees, "Why Americans Must Oppose the PLO." *The Review of the News*, October 17, 1979.

Joseph Farah, "Roadmap to Nowhere." *World Net Daily*, May 6, 2003.

Martin A. Lee, "The Swastika and the Crescent."

Nissan Ratzlav-Katz, "We Didn't Start the Fire." *National Review Online*, August 23, 2002.

Phillip Mattar, *The Mufti of Jerusalem* (New York: Columbia University Press, 1988), 101.

Robert Fox, "Albanians and Afghans Fight for Heirs of Bosnia's SS Party." *Daily Telegraph*, December 29, 1993 .

Susan Rosenbluth, "Imam: Koran Says Jews Are Supposed to Return to Israel." *The Jewish Voice and Opinion*, March 2003.

William Ziff, *The Rape of Palestine* (New York: Greenwood, 1975), 22.

"Who Was the Grand Mufti, Haj Muhammed Amin al-Husseini?" *Palestine Facts*, www.palestinefacts.org/pf_mandate_grand_mufti.php.

Zvi Elpeleg, *The Grand Mufti: Haj al-Husseini, Founder of the Palestinian National Movement* (Portland, Oregon: Frank Cass, 1993), 4.

Index